The Gambling Problem

ISSUES

Volume 203

Series Editor
Lisa Firth

Independence
Educational Publishers
Cambridge

First published by Independence

The Studio, High Green

Great Shelford

Cambridge CB22 5EG

England

British Library Cataloguing in Publication Data

The gambling problem. -- (Issues ; v. 203)

1. Gambling--Great Britain. 2. Compulsive gamblers--Great Britain.

I. Series II. Firth, Lisa.

363.4'2'0941-dc22

ISBN-13: 978 1 86168 575 9

Printed in Great Britain

MWL Print Group Ltd

CONTENTS

Chapter 1 Gambling Trends

Chapter 2 Young People and Gambling

Chapter 3 Problem Gambling

OTHER TITLES IN THE ISSUES SERIES

For more on these titles, visit: www.independence.co.uk

Stress and Anxiety ISBN 978 1 86168 314 4
Customers and Consumerism ISBN 978 1 86168 386 1
A Genetically Modified Future? ISBN 978 1 86168 390 8
The Education Problem ISBN 978 1 86168 391 5
Vegetarian and Vegan Diets ISBN 978 1 86168 406 6
Media Issues ISBN 978 1 86168 408 0
The Cloning Debate ISBN 978 1 86168 410 3
Sustainability and Environment ISBN 978 1 86168 419 6
The Terrorism Problem ISBN 978 1 86168 420 2
Religious Beliefs ISBN 978 1 86168 421 9
A Classless Society? ISBN 978 1 86168 422 6
Migration and Population ISBN 978 1 86168 423 3
Climate Change ISBN 978 1 86168 424 0
Euthanasia and the Right to Die ISBN 978 1 86168 439 4
Sexual Orientation and Society ISBN 978 1 86168 440 0
The Gender Gap ISBN 978 1 86168 441 7
Domestic Abuse ISBN 978 1 86168 442 4
Travel and Tourism ISBN 978 1 86168 443 1
The Problem of Globalisation ISBN 978 1 86168 444 8
The Internet Revolution ISBN 978 1 86168 451 6
An Ageing Population ISBN 978 1 86168 452 3
Poverty and Exclusion ISBN 978 1 86168 453 0
Waste Issues ISBN 978 1 86168 454 7
Staying Fit ISBN 978 1 86168 455 4
Drugs in the UK ISBN 978 1 86168 456 1
The AIDS Crisis ISBN 978 1 86168 468 4
Bullying Issues ISBN 978 1 86168 469 1
Marriage and Cohabitation ISBN 978 1 86168 470 7
Our Human Rights ISBN 978 1 86168 471 4
Privacy and Surveillance ISBN 978 1 86168 472 1
The Animal Rights Debate ISBN 978 1 86168 473 8
Body Image and Self-Esteem ISBN 978 1 86168 484 4
Abortion – Rights and Ethics ISBN 978 1 86168 485 1
Racial and Ethnic Discrimination ISBN 978 1 86168 486 8
Sexual Health ISBN 978 1 86168 487 5
Selling Sex ISBN 978 1 86168 488 2
Citizenship and Participation ISBN 978 1 86168 489 9
Health Issues for Young People ISBN 978 1 86168 500 1
Crime in the UK ISBN 978 1 86168 501 8
Reproductive Ethics ISBN 978 1 86168 502 5
Tackling Child Abuse ISBN 978 1 86168 503 2
Money and Finances ISBN 978 1 86168 504 9
The Housing Issue ISBN 978 1 86168 505 6
Teenage Conceptions ISBN 978 1 86168 523 0
Work and Employment ISBN 978 1 86168 524 7
Understanding Eating Disorders ISBN 978 1 86168 525 4
Student Matters ISBN 978 1 86168 526 1
Cannabis Use ISBN 978 1 86168 527 8
Health and the State ISBN 978 1 86168 528 5
Tobacco and Health ISBN 978 1 86168 539 1
The Homeless Population ISBN 978 1 86168 540 7
Coping with Depression ISBN 978 1 86168 541 4
The Changing Family ISBN 978 1 86168 542 1
Bereavement and Grief ISBN 978 1 86168 543 8
Endangered Species ISBN 978 1 86168 544 5
Responsible Drinking ISBN 978 1 86168 555 1
Alternative Medicine ISBN 978 1 86168 560 5
Censorship Issues ISBN 978 1 86168 558 2
Living with Disability ISBN 978 1 86168 557 5
Sport and Society ISBN 978 1 86168 559 9
Self-Harming and Suicide ISBN 978 1 86168 556 8
Sustainable Transport ISBN 978 1 86168 572 8
Mental Wellbeing ISBN 978 1 86168 573 5
Child Exploitation ISBN 978 1 86168 574 2
The Gambling Problem ISBN 978 1 86168 575 9
The Energy Crisis ISBN 978 1 86168 576 6
Nutrition and Diet ISBN 978 1 86168 577 3

A note on critical evaluation

Because the information reprinted here is from a number of different sources, readers should bear in mind the origin of the text and whether the source is likely to have a particular bias when presenting information (just as they would if undertaking their own research). It is hoped that, as you read about the many aspects of the issues explored in this book, you will critically evaluate the information presented. It is important that you decide whether you are being presented with facts or opinions. Does the writer give a biased or an unbiased report? If an opinion is being expressed, do you agree with the writer?

The Gambling Problem offers a useful starting point for those who need convenient access to information about the many issues involved. However, it is only a starting point. Following each article is a URL to the relevant organisation's website, which you may wish to visit for further information.

Chapter 1 **GAMBLING TRENDS**

Understanding gambling

Problem gambling is when harm occurs because of gambling. This harm may take many forms and can extend to other people in the gambler's life.

Gambling – how does it start?

Gambling doesn't start as a problem.

For most people it starts out as a good thing: for example, as:

- Time away from the pressures of work and family;
- An opportunity to get away from thoughts and feelings which may be depressing;
- A bit of excitement;
- A dream of winning a fortune;
- An opportunity to get out and socialise;
- Feeling that a gambling venue is a safe place to go, no matter what the time.

Gambling can change and grow without people noticing how it has become more important.

A significant change or stress is commonly the trigger for gambling to escalate out of control. A big win can also have the same effect. Even without specific stress, gambling can increase. People often find that they have to gamble with increasing amounts of money to achieve satisfaction. Also, gambling, through its increasing demands on time, energy and money, creates other stresses in people's relationships, work and finances.

Why do people gamble?

Individuals who have gambling problems most often ask this question. They are unable to understand how, when they know gambling is causing them problems, they just don't or can't stop. It just doesn't make sense!

Life stress can also cause pain, emotional pain, and consequently other responses such as anxiety, boredom and depression

Rather than asking 'why' individuals gamble, perhaps it is better to understand 'how' gambling fits into people's lives. What part does it play? What need does it satisfy?

Most people who have problems with gambling fall into two broad groups:

- Those that say they gamble because it gives them some excitement and is challenging; and
- Those who, while gambling, experience times when they don't think or feel. It is like a numbing experience, where their worries and cares disappear and their problems are forgotten.

A process of gambling

Let's present a different way of thinking about gambling. When we are in physical pain, we do something to alleviate the pain: for example, take a paracetamol.

STATE OF VICTORIA

Life stress can also cause pain, emotional pain, and consequently other responses such as anxiety, boredom and depression. We may find other things to do to alleviate emotional pain, for example talking to friends, drinking, taking drugs or gambling.

Just like medication, gambling can offer some emotional pain relief. To medicate their pain, people may turn to gambling. Gambling can also introduce other factors which begin a cycle for the gambler that is difficult to get out of.

The cost of gambling

When thinking about gambling it is important to recognise that uncontrolled gambling causes more than just financial harm. It may also negatively affect other aspects of a gambler's life, for example:

- Losing the respect of family, friends and work colleagues.
- Losing self-respect.
- Relationships with others, for example losing contact with friends.
- Health, for example not eating or sleeping properly, existing health problems becoming worse.
- Work performance, for example absence from work, inability to concentrate.
- The likelihood of committing illegal activities, for example stealing.
- Social activities, for example losing interest in, and the ability to, go out.
- Ability to engage in educational activities.

When gambling becomes a problem

There is no certain answer to when gambling becomes a problem. It is up to the individual to decide whether there is a problem or not. The following things might happen if someone has a problem with gambling:

- Shopping money is used for gambling.
- There is no spare money to spend on themselves.
- Money for bills is spent on gambling.
- The truth about their gambling behaviour is hidden or lied about.
- Other people are relied on for financial assistance.
- Loss of interest in family and friends.
- Work is missed to spend time gambling.
- Increased fights at home to have an excuse to go out and gamble.
- Temptation to take someone else's money to gamble with.
- Inability to stop gambling.
- Finding excuses for gambling losses.
- There are more gambling debts on credit cards than purchases.
- Eating and sleeping are neglected in favour of gambling.

One thing we know about problem gambling is that some of the things people believe about gambling may push them to gamble more.

Some people who develop problems with gambling believe:

- If they continue gambling, they are bound to win soon.
- If they continue gambling, they will win back what they have lost.
- That gambling is a solution to financial problems.
- That gambling is the only immediate escape from stress.
- That the only way to stop urges to gamble is to gamble.

None of these beliefs are true.

July 2009

- Reproduced with permission from the Victorian State Government, from www.problemgambling.vic.gov.au

STATE OF VICTORIA

Gambling participation

Information from the Gambling Commission.

Introduction

This article provides information on participation in gambling. It sets out the findings from questions asked through telephone omnibus surveys conducted by ICM Research. The results presented in this article are from two separate, but complementary, sets of questions: one measuring participation in all types of gambling and one which monitors participation solely in remote gambling.

Questions monitoring participation in all types of gambling activity have been asked in their current form since June 2008. These results were first published in January 2010, and will continue to be published on a quarterly basis. Questions on remote gambling have been included for a longer period and are also published on a quarterly basis.

Methodology

Each survey is conducted once a quarter (in March, June, September and December) with a nationally representative sample (in terms of age, gender, social classification and region) of adults (over-18-year-olds). To ensure consistency and comparability, both surveys usually take place at the same time of the week in each quarter. The overall sample size is relatively robust, especially when measured on a regular basis over time. However, when analysing specific forms or methods of gambling, the sample numbers are lower, with consequential increased margins of error in the percentages given. Where figures do not add up to 100% it is because respondents refused to answer, answered 'don't know' or were permitted to give multiple responses.

In order to minimise sample volatility, all the data contained within this report are shown as annual figures by averaging the results for four quarterly surveys. Up to June 2010 the survey questions were each asked of 2,000 respondents each quarter: thus the four quarter average figures were previously based on a sample size of 8,000 respondents. From September 2010, each set of questions are asked of 1,000 respondents per quarter. This means that the reported sample size will decline by 1,000 respondents each quarter for each set of questions, until June 2011 when all subsequent reports will be based on 4,000 respondents (for each set of questions). Therefore, the results in this report for the year to September 2010 are based on 7,000 respondents. A full breakdown of base sizes is available in the annex to the full report.

Key findings

The following findings are based on two separate sets of questions commissioned by the Gambling Commission in omnibus surveys conducted by ICM Research. The first set of questions measures participation in all types of gambling activity (including by remote means); the second set measures participation in remote forms of gambling (that is, gambling through a computer, mobile phone or interactive/digital TV).

All gambling participation (including by remote means)

- Over the year to September 2010 (that is, an average of figures for December 2009, March 2010, June 2010 and September 2010), 54.3% of the 7,000 adults surveyed said they had participated in at least one form of gambling in the previous four weeks.
- This figure of 54.3% compares with the 2009 calendar year figure of 55.2%.
- The most popular gambling activity was National Lottery tickets (45.0% of respondents), followed by tickets for society or other good cause lotteries (10.7%) and National Lottery Scratchcards (10.1%). Betting on horse races, private betting and gaming with family and friends, and the football pools were the next most popular activities (3.4%, 3.1% and 3.1%, respectively).

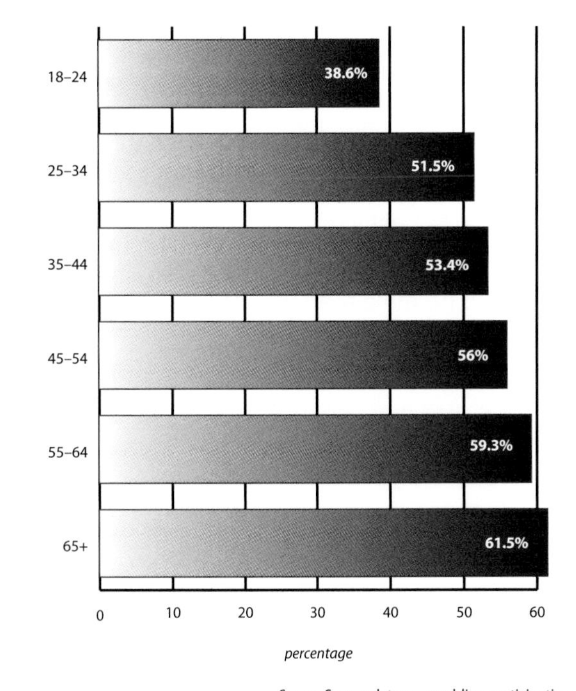

GAMBLING COMMISSION

- Those participating in gambling were more likely to be male than female, and were more likely to be aged over 45.

Remote gambling participation

- Over the year to September 2010 (that is, an average of figures for December 2009, March 2010, June 2010 and September 2010), 10.5% of the 7,000 adults surveyed said they had participated in at least one form of remote gambling in the previous four weeks. Around half of these had participated just in National Lottery products.
- This figure of 10.5% compares with the 2009 calendar year figure which was also 10.5%, the 2008 calendar year figure of 9.7%, the 2007 calendar year figure of 8.8% and the 2006 calendar year figure of 7.2%.

Remote gambling via a computer, laptop or handheld device was most popular (9.4% of all respondents), followed by gambling via mobile phone (2.7%)

- The growth in participation in remote gambling is explained very largely by increased online participation in the National Lottery. If those only playing National Lottery products remotely are excluded, 5.7% of respondents had participated in remote gambling in the year to September 2010, compared with the same figure of 5.7% in 2009, 5.6% in 2008, 5.2% in 2007 and 5.1% in 2006.
- Overall, in the year to September 2010, 8.3% of respondents said they had remotely purchased tickets for the National Lottery draw in the previous four weeks (either only or in addition to other types of gambling activity).
- Those participating in remote gambling were more likely to be male than female, and were more likely to be aged 18–44.
- Remote gambling via a computer, laptop or handheld device was most popular (9.5% of all respondents), followed by gambling via mobile phone (2.7%) and interactive/digital TV (1.4%).

October 2010

- The above information is an extract from the Gambling Commission's report *Survey data on gambling participation*, and is reprinted with permission. Visit www.gamblingcommission.gov.uk for more information.

GAMBLING COMMISSION / GAMBLE AWARE

Types of gambling

Almost three-quarters of the adult population in the United Kingdom gamble in some way each year.

Betting

A bet is a gamble in which a player stakes money on the outcome of an event; for example, who will win the World Cup or a general election.

Bingo

Bingo is a game of chance where players receive a set of numbers on a card in return for a stake and they mark them off as a caller announces numbers drawn randomly.

Casino games

Casino games include table, card and machine games played in a casino. They involve playing or staking against a bank. Traditional casino games include roulette, blackjack and poker.

Gaming machines

Fruit machines, fixed-odds betting terminals, slot machines, pusher and crane-grab machines are all gaming machines. The player generally wins by matching the symbols, usually fruit, on the central line of three reels.

Lotteries

A lottery is a game which people enter by selecting a set of numbers that may match those drawn later for the chance of winning money or prizes.

Pools

In pools betting, players 'pool' their stakes and the combined sum, less what the operator takes out, is divided between the winning participants.

Spread betting

Spread betting allows people to bet on sporting events, politics or stock market movements.

- The above information is reprinted with kind permission from Gamble Aware. Visit www.gambleaware.co.uk for more information.

What is gambling?

Information from GamCare.

Actually there is no single, clear-cut definition of what gambling is but it is widely agreed that:

- Two or more people agree to take part in the activity (usually an operator and the person who wishes to gamble).
- Normally money (the 'stake') is paid by the loser to the winner.
- The outcome is uncertain.
- The result is determined at least partly by chance.
- Participation is an active experience but can be avoided by not taking part.

A brief history

- 2000 BC – Egyptians used knucklebones as four-sided dice.
- 1500 BC – in China, spinning discs were used to play an early roulette game.
- 210 AD – the first recorded horse race took place in England.
- 1588 – the first lottery was approved in Britain by Elizabeth I to raise money to repair the Cinque Ports.
- 1895 – Charles Fey, a mechanic from San Francisco produced the first slot machine.
- 1906 – gambling in public was prohibited by the Street Betting Act.
- 1926 – the first greyhound race in Britain was held in Manchester; Winston Churchill imposed a betting tax (abolished three years later).
- 1960 – the Betting and Gaming Act legalised betting shops in Britain. Before this there was widespread illegal gambling.

1926 – the first greyhound race in Britain was held in Manchester; Winston Churchill imposed a betting tax (abolished three years later)

- 1964 – Gamblers Anonymous was founded in the UK (having originated in America).
- 1994 – the National Lottery was launched.
- 1995 – Lottery Scratchcards were introduced.
- 1996 – for the first time betting shops were allowed to have (a maximum of two) fruit machines.
- 2007 – the UK Government introduced the Gambling Act 2005 .

- The above information is reprinted with kind permission from GamCare. Visit www.gamcare.org for more information.

Gambling participation by type of gambling activity, 2009

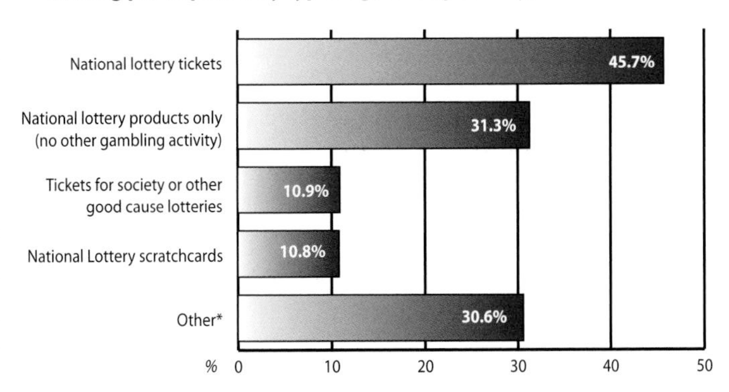

** Responses included in the Other category have individual values of 4% or less and include: Betting on horse races with a bookmaker; Private betting; playing cards/games for money with family, friends or colleagues; The football pools; Bingo cards/tickets at bingo hall; Fruit or slot machines; Online betting with a bookmaker on any event or sport; Betting on other events or sports with a bookmaker (does not include online); Virtual gaming machines in a bookmaker's; Betting exchanges; Online gambling other than betting (includes poker, bingo, slot machine and casino style games); Table games in a casino; Organised poker in clubs and pubs; Betting on dog races or virtual dog races with a bookmaker (does not include online); Spread betting; Any other gambling activity; Don't know.*

Remote gambling participation by method, 2009

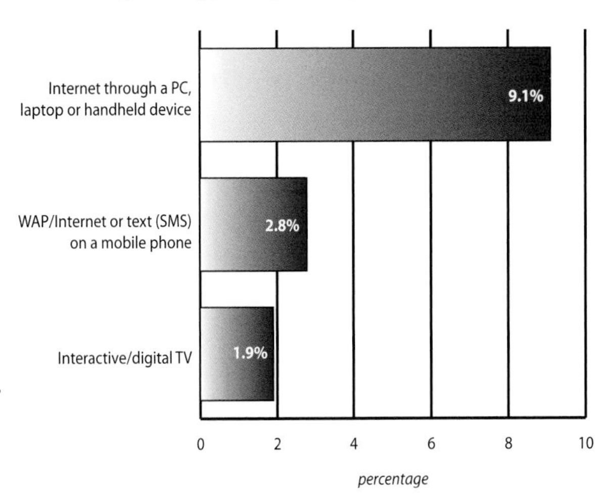

Source: Survey data on gambling participation, 2009, © *The Gambling Commission. All rights reserved*

GAMCARE

FAQ: gambling and you

What's a gambling addiction and how can you tell if you or someone you know has a problem? TheSite.org spoke to Adrian Scarfe, Head of Clinical Services at GamCare.

What is a gambling addiction?

It's when the urges to gamble are so strong that you do it even though you know it's going to damage your health and cause financial problems. Many people say they can't stop gambling from the moment they get up to the moment they go to bed. Some are so ashamed of their gambling they hide it away from others. Often the financial stress of gambling is overwhelming and you've got yourself into so much debt that you feel the only way to get out of it is to continue to gamble. The most serious aspect of gambling is when you 'chase your losses'. This is when you start losing and desperately try to win back your money by continuing to gamble, only to end up with more losses.

Who is most likely to be affected by gambling?

Gambling can affect anyone, at any age, whether you've got money or not. At GamCare, we speak to people who have virtually no money because of their gambling and find themselves on the street or facing a marriage break-up. We also have high-powered professional people who get into difficulties with gambling. People between the ages of 16 and 24 are four times more likely to develop a gambling problem than any other age group. Young people are also more vulnerable to Internet and mobile phone gambling.

Gambling can affect anyone, at any age... People between the ages of 16 and 24 are four times more likely to develop a gambling problem than any other age group. Young people are also more vulnerable to Internet and mobile phone gambling

What are the temptations to gamble?

If you compare gambling to smoking, which is an equally powerful addiction, you could say it's easier to give up smoking. Smoking has been banned in many public places and there are numerous ads telling you how bad it is for you. The publicity surrounding gambling is the opposite, with adverts encouraging you to gamble. There is the National Lottery, sports and quiz programmes, and the Internet is available 24/7. These are huge triggers, so if you've got a gambling addiction it's getting increasingly difficult to escape from it.

How can gambling be a healthy hobby?

If you have a bet or go out for a night, when you win, be happy and walk away. Don't see it as a way of making money or as a way of increasing your self-esteem. It's simply a form of entertainment, and that's the healthy way to gamble. The unhealthy aspect of gambling is when you're seeing it as an easy or quick way to make money – it's not. Over a long period of time you can't win at gambling because the odds are always stacked against you. This is the reason why casinos and betting shops make so much money. The second unhealthy aspect of gambling is when you do it in order to make yourself feel better about yourself. You may start feeling better at the beginning, but you could end up feeling a lot worse. The third aspect is when you're gambling as a way of escaping your problems, rather than addressing the issues.

How will giving up gambling affect an addict?

What is not well known, even among people with a gambling addiction, is that you can get withdrawal symptoms just as if you're coming off drugs, alcohol or cigarettes, even though there's no actual substance in you that's making you gamble. There may be a feeling of restlessness and a sense of not knowing what to do with your time, which can make you feel you've got to have another bet. There could also be disturbed sleep, mood swings, headaches or other stress-induced symptoms such as IBS. At the same time there are people who can just walk away from it and not go through any of these symptoms.

How can you stop gambling in the first place?

It's not always a matter of trying to reduce gambling – if you've got a severe addiction you should have some time away before you consider going back into a controlled gambling situation, and not everyone can do that. A lot of people when they have an addiction will either not know it, or will be in what counsellors call 'denial', where they are actually saying that they can stop if they need to, they just don't want to. If

THESITE.ORG

there is a family member or a friend who is showing the signs, the best thing you can do is say very gently and sensitively: 'I'm not saying you've got a problem, but why don't you talk to someone and see if you do.' That would be the encouragement they may need to get some support and professional help.

If you have a bet or go out for a night, when you win, be happy and walk away. Don't see it as a way of making money or as a way of increasing your self-esteem

How can you deal with a relapse?

If you've been trying to stop and you go back to gambling, don't treat it as a disaster and worry that you've messed up and are back to square one. Learn from the mistake you've made and understand why you did it, and then put the lessons you've learnt into action. In moments of despair, like anything else, always get someone to talk it through with you and share your burden – preferably professionals, but if you can't, a trusted friend.

⇨ The above information is reprinted with kind permission from TheSite.org. Visit www.thesite.org for more information.

Why a healthy brain is no good for gambling

Brain damage can give gamblers an edge in certain circumstances, a study shows.

By Marc Abrahams

Brain damage can sometimes give gamblers a winning edge, an American study suggests. The researchers take a flier at explaining how and why certain brain lesions might, in some circumstances, help a person to triumph over others or over adversity.

The study – 'Investment Behavior and the Negative Side of Emotion' – published in the journal *Psychological Science*, renders its tantalising, juicy question into lofty academese. The five co-authors, led by Baba Shiv, a marketing professor at Stanford University, ask: 'Can dysfunction in neural systems subserving emotion lead, under certain circumstances, to more advantageous decisions?'

The team experimented with people who had abnormalities in particular brain regions – the amygdala, the orbitofrontal cortex, and the right insular or somatosensory cortex. Medically, those can be a sign that something's amiss in how the person handles emotions.

Each brain-damaged person got a wad of play money, and instructions to gamble on 20 rounds of coin-tossing (heads-you-win/tails-you-lose, with some added twists). Other people who had no such brain lesions got the same money and the same gambling instructions.

The brain-damaged gamblers pretty consistently ended up with more money than their healthier-brained competitors. The researchers speculate that when 'normal' gamblers encounter a run of unhappy coin-toss results, they get discouraged and become cautious – perhaps too cautious. Not so the people with brain-lesion-induced emotional disfunction. Encountering a run of bad luck, they plough on, undaunted. And then enjoy a relatively handsome payoff. At least sometimes.

The study notes that this brain damage side-benefit might occasionally even save someone's life.

They cite the case of a man with ventromedial prefrontal damage who was driving under hazardous road conditions: 'When other drivers reached an icy patch, they hit their brakes in panic, causing their vehicles to skid out of control, but the patient crossed the icy patch unperturbed, gently pulling away from a tailspin and driving ahead safely. The patient remembered the fact that not hitting the brakes was the appropriate behaviour, and his lack of fear allowed him to perform optimally.'

Shiv has an eye for non-standard ways of exploring human behaviour. He sometimes teaches a course called The Frinky Science of the Mind.

In 2008, he and three colleagues were awarded an Ig Nobel prize for demonstrating that expensive fake medicine is more effective than cheap fake medicine.

27 September 2010

Gambling on the up, says Sportingbet

Online gaming firm Sportingbet says more of us are betting on live sporting events as it announced revenues were up by nearly a third in the last year.

By Harry Glass and PA

A £50m betting spree on World Cup matches helped lift overall sales to £208m, thanks to several favoured teams losing matches.

The Channel Islands-based firm said 'in play' gaming – live betting during an event – accounted for 61% of its core sports betting business in the year to July, up from 56% last year.

Andrew McIver, Sportingbet chief executive, said revenues were 27% higher in its most recent financial year and are up 17% in the first two months this time round.

The company reported a fall in pre-tax profits to £6.9m from £22.3m in the year, but this included a £22.8m settlement with the US Department of Justice over an investigation into alleged illegal Internet gambling.

The company, which operates across Europe and in Australia, said the total amounts wagered for the year grew by 25% to £1.9bn

The agreement, which analysts have said clears the way for potential mergers or takeovers, means the firm will avoid being prosecuted in the US for accepting online bets made by Americans between 1998 and 2006.

The company, which operates across Europe and in Australia, said the total amounts wagered for the year grew by 25% to £1.9bn.

Betting on sports is the group's core business, accounting for 69% of revenue, compared to 64% last year.

Football is the core product, accounting for 43% of revenue, but the company said it had invested in other sports such as horse racing and tennis.

The firm said 'competitive and economic pressures' were hampering its casino, games and poker offering, which account for a third of the business. Games include Virtual Dogs, Wheel of Fortune and Championship Manager, and all involve betting.

Casino sales were up in the year from £41.3m to £44.9m, while poker revenues were down from £18.8m to £17.4m.

Ivor Jones, analyst at Numis Securities, said the strong performance and settlement with the US Department of Justice 'clears the decks' for a potential takeover of the firm. Shares were up 3% following the results.

He said: 'We expect Sportingbet to be involved in merger and acquisition activity within the next 12 months, and this encourages us to be very positive on the shares.'

Potential buyers have been highlighted as bwin and PartyGaming, who agreed to merge in July under a £1bn agreement.

6 October 2010

⇨ The above information is reprinted with kind permission from Thisismoney.co.uk

THISISMONEY

Youth gambling and problem gambling

Information from the International Centre for Youth Gambling Problems and High-Risk Behaviors.

Although problem gambling has been primarily thought of as an adult behaviour, gambling activities appear to be particularly attractive to today's youth. In fact, prevalence studies conducted in the United States, Canada, New Zealand, Europe and Australia have noted rising prevalence rates of youth involvement in both legal and illegal forms of gambling. While approximately 60% of adolescents report having gambled for money during the past year, 4–8% of adolescents presently have a serious gambling problem with another 10–14% of adolescents at risk for developing a serious gambling problem. Yet, for most parents and teens, gambling is viewed as an innocuous behaviour with few negative consequences.

When do youths begin gambling?

Gambling has become a widely accepted activity in many cultures. It is not unusual for parents to purchase lottery tickets for their children or to take them to play bingo. Retrospective studies found that adult problem gamblers reported an earlier onset of gambling, often beginning between the ages of ten to 19, with some studies showing children as young as nine years old beginning gambling. Similar results were found in several of our studies, as well as in other studies conducted throughout the world.

Negative consequences associated with adolescent problem gambling

Problematic gambling among adolescents has been linked with increased delinquency and criminal behaviour, as well as the disruption of family and peer relationships. Problem gambling can also negatively affect overall school performance and work activities. While youths may present with different initial symptoms than adults, they nevertheless share similar characteristics. For example, adolescent problem gamblers report a preoccupation with gambling, sacrificing school, work, parental and peer relationships in order to continue gambling.

Reasons for gambling

Contrary to public opinion, our research and clinical work suggests that money is not the only reason why adolescents gamble excessively. Rather, it appears that money is used as a vehicle which enables individuals to continue playing. When playing, adolescents with serious gambling problems report that nothing else matters and that they are able to forget about their problems. The three predominant reasons adolescents report gambling are (a) the excitement it brings, (b) enjoyment and (c) to win money. Other reasons adolescents may gamble include peer pressure and to relieve feelings of depression. Some of our recent research suggests that youths also engage in gambling to relieve their boredom.

Problematic gambling among adolescents has been linked with increased delinquency and criminal behaviour, as well as the disruption of family and peer relationships

What has research taught us about adolescents with serious gambling problems?

Adolescent problem gamblers:

- are more likely to be boys but girls seem to be catching up;
- are overly represented as a group compared to adult problem gamblers;
- are greater risk-takers in general;
- often show signs of lower self-esteem;
- tend to report higher rates of depression;
- often gamble to escape problems;
- are more likely to develop an addiction;

INTERNATIONAL CENTRE FOR YOUTH GAMBLING PROBLEMS AND HIGH-RISK BEHAVIORS

- ➪ seem to be more excitable and outgoing;
- ➪ are more anxious and less self-disciplined;
- ➪ are at greater risk for suicide ideation and suicide attempts;
- ➪ often replace their regular friends with gambling acquaintances;
- ➪ have poor general coping skills;
- ➪ report beginning gambling at an early age (approximately ten);
- ➪ often recall an early big win;
- ➪ report more daily hassles and major traumatic life events;
- ➪ often have parents, relatives or friends who gamble;
- ➪ are more likely to be delinquent and involved in criminal activities to acquire money;
- ➪ develop problems with family and friends;
- ➪ move quickly from just gambling with friends and family to problem gambling;
- ➪ show decreased academic performance.

➪ The above information is reprinted with kind permission from the International Centre for Youth Gambling Problems and High-Risk Behaviors. Visit their website at www.youthgambling.mcgill.ca for more information.

Kids speak out about gambling

Personal stories from International Centre for Youth Gambling Problems and High-Risk Behaviors.

'The casino was open all the time, and I know that any time I needed to be somewhere, there would be people there and something exciting for me to do. I went when I didn't feel like going to class, when I didn't want to be at home. I went when I had a lot of work to do because for the time I was sitting at the table I forgot about my work. I don't like going there with people anymore. I just want to be alone and be able to do my thing. I was happy there.' *Female, age 18*

'I can't expect any of my friends to understand what is going on.' *Male, age 17*

'I want to jump out of a plane… I think it would give me a similar rush.' *Female, age 18*

'I made gambling more important than anything else.' *Male, age 18*

'It was a game in the beginning, then I used it to kill time, then I realised it was a great escape." *Male, age 17*

'What keeps me from going back is remembering how sick I was… I was not a real person any more.' *Female, age 19*

'When I lose, it's really good because I am on a mission… I have something to do…try to win my money back.' *Male, age 18*

'No, money wasn't the reason for my gambling. But just like cars use gas, I used money.' *Female, age 19*

'When I was gambling, I woke up every day thinking this was going to be a big day.' *Male, age 17*

➪ The above information is reprinted with kind permission from the International Centre for Youth Gambling. Visit www.youthgambling.mcgill.ca for more information.

GamCare targets teen gambling

2% of adolescents – 60,000 12- to 15-year-olds – are problem gamblers. Yet only 5% of parents would stop their child from gambling.

Nothing in the school curriculum helps children understand the risks and how to manage them, and there is no coherent national strategy to address this.

These are the findings brought together by GamCare, the leading national provider of support, advice and treatment for problem gambling, in a report published today. *Beating the odds: preventing teenage problem gambling* sets out GamCare's programme for action.

Minister for Tourism and Heritage John Penrose, who has responsibility in the Government for gambling policy, said:

'GamCare have highlighted an important issue. Better education for the young, and for parents, is key to preventing problems later in life. Many people enjoy gambling as a sociable leisure activity, but helping young people to understand how to gamble responsibly and to make informed choices is vital to ensuring we keep gambling safe and fun.'

'When it's out of control, gambling can lead to dropping out of school, depression, and turning to alcohol or drugs to cope'

Rt Hon David Willetts MP, Minister for Universities and Science, comments:

'Educating young people about the risks of gambling is vital. Students can be a particularly vulnerable group. If, before they arrive at university, they are equipped with an awareness of the risks and the strategies to stay in control, they'll be able to make wiser decisions.'

GamCare's ambassador, Chris Eubank, says:

'I know only too well from my own experience how easy it is when you are young to get drawn into things without being aware of the consequences. Problem gambling is not just about losing your money – or someone else's. When it's out of control, gambling can lead to dropping out of school, depression, and turning to alcohol or drugs to cope. Some are tempted into crime to pay their debts. Some consider ending their lives. I'll be lending my weight to GamCare's efforts across the country, particularly with disadvantaged young people.'

GamCare CEO Andy McLellan says:

'This is the first time the latest UK statistics and international evidence has been brought together. The facts that emerge point to an urgent need to inform young people – and their parents – about responsible gambling, and to provide help for those already in trouble. GamCare, with its partners, is developing a programme and materials for use in schools, youth centres and elsewhere to address the issue. We'll harness new channels of communication aimed specifically at a young audience, both to raise awareness and to deliver help and support for anyone in trouble. We want problem gambling to be talked about frankly and openly, with easily understood messages. Under-18s aren't seeking our help at the moment and we need to encourage more of them to talk to us now, rather than hold back until a potential crisis point later in life.'

'Under-18s aren't seeking our help at the moment and we need to encourage more of them to talk to us now'

GamCare's planned programme includes:

- Pilots in different regions bringing expert counsellors, teachers, parents and voluntary groups together to raise awareness locally.
- Development of new ways to communicate with and help young people, using social networking, viral advertising, mobile content, etc.
- Short and accessible training packages for teachers, youth workers and others working with young people to increase their awareness of the issues and of how to find help.

We can make a start thanks to specific donations from the private sector. We're keen to work with others to make the programme a reality.

28 September 2010

➪ The above information is reprinted with kind permission from GamCare. Please visit www.gamcare.org.uk for more information.

GAMCARE

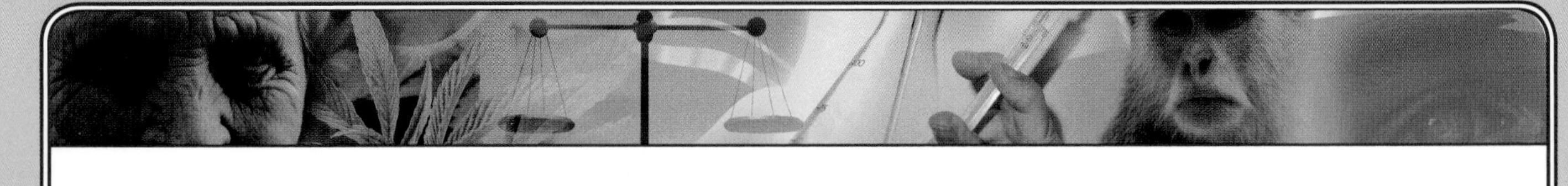

Children, the National Lottery and gambling 2008–09

Summary report of a quantitative survey.

Introduction

The 2008–09 British Survey of Children and Gambling was carried out by Ipsos MORI's Social Research Institute and the Centre for the Study of Gambling at the University of Salford on behalf of the National Lottery Commission. The research consisted of a quantitative survey of nearly 9,000 children aged between 12 and 15 in England and Wales. Children filled out self-completion questionnaires which captured information about their experiences of, and attitudes towards, gambling on a range of games. Questionnaires were administered via schools; overall a school-level response rate of 22% was achieved.

The research consisted of a quantitative survey of nearly 9,000 children aged between 12 and 15 in England and Wales

This research study uses the same methodology, and covers similar topics, as surveys conducted in 1997, 1999, 2000 and 2005–06.

Please note that throughout the report, reference is made to 'problem' and 'social' gamblers. Problem gambling, or pathological gambling, is defined by the American Psychiatric Association as 'persistent and recurrent maladaptive gambling behaviour that disrupts personal, family, or vocational pursuits', gambling that becomes a compulsion despite the negative consequences it causes. Social gambling is defined as, 'gambling which lasts for a limited amount of time with predetermined acceptable losses'. The survey uses the DSM-IV-MR-J screen to identify whether respondents who gamble are problem or social gamblers.

Key findings

Rates of past week gambling

The proportion of children buying National Lottery tickets with their own money in the seven days preceding their interview has fallen significantly in recent years. In the current survey two per cent had played Lotto in the past seven days – down from five per cent in 2005–06 – and four per cent had bought scratchcards (down from six per cent in 2005–06).

In line with the decline in the proportion of children actually spending money on National Lottery games, the proportion of children trying to buy tickets is also on a downward trend: two per cent of children attempted to buy National Lottery tickets in the past seven days, compared with five per cent in 2005–06; and four per cent tried to buy Scratchcards, down from eight per cent in 2005–06.

Rates of gambling on other commercial and non-commercial forms of gambling have also fallen over time. One-fifth (21 per cent) of children had gambled (on any type of game) in the past seven days, down from 26 per cent in 2005–06. Most significantly, rates of playing slot machines – although still higher than other forms of gambling among children – have fallen sharply from 17 per cent in 2005–06 to nine per cent currently. This fall coincides with the increasingly limited availability of these machines following the introduction of new legislation.

Levels of problem gambling

Levels of problem gambling among young gamblers was assessed using a youth-adapted problem gambling screen (DSM-IV-MR-J). Rates of problem gambling have fallen since 2005–06: two per cent of children were identified as problem gamblers compared with 3.5 per cent in 2005–06. It is likely that this drop reflects falling levels of gambling among children over time, particularly on potentially more addictive forms of gambling such as slot machines.

One-fifth (21 per cent) ofchildren had gambled (on anytype of game) in the past seven days down from 26 per cent in 2005–06

Deterrents to purchasing National Lottery tickets or Scratchcards

When asked what would deter them from buying National Lottery tickets, a third (34 per cent) of young gamblers say being asked to prove they were over 16 would be off-putting. However, among those who were refused when trying to buy a National Lottery ticket in the past seven days, 30 per cent say they were refused once, 19 per cent say they were refused twice, and 28 per cent were refused more than twice, suggesting that some children will persistently try to buy tickets, even if they are initially refused.

IPSOS MORI

Where do children buy National Lottery tickets and Scratchcards?

Children are most likely to buy their National Lottery tickets and Scratchcards at corner shops and newsagents (62 per cent of those who had bought in the past seven days used these outlets, which equates to two per cent of all children buying tickets in these outlets), while supermarkets and other retailers are used much less frequently, suggesting that regulatory focus on this type of outlet may be of greatest value in tackling under-age play.

Awareness of gambling advertising

More than three-quarters (78 per cent) of children recall recently seeing television adverts or Internet pop-ups relating to the National Lottery and other gambling like poker, bingo and sports betting.

Those who had gambled in the past seven days (84 per cent) and those who had played free gambling games online (82 per cent) were more likely than average (78 per cent) to recall seeing gambling advertisements. Children who engaged in other illegal behaviours were also more likely than average to recall seeing gambling advertisements: for example, 82 per cent who had taken illegal drugs and 83 per cent who had played truant remembered these advertisements. The findings highlight the value of closely monitoring these types of advertisements to limit their potential appeal to under-age players as far as possible.

Characteristics of past-week gamblers and non-gamblers

	Percentage of respondents who had gambled in the past seven days	Percentage of respondents who had not gambled in the past seven days
Gender: male	28%	69%
Gender: female	13%	84%
Year group: 8	20%	77%
Year group: 10	22%	75%
Ethnicity: White	21%	76%
Ethnicity: Asian	14%	73%
Ethnicity: Black	23%	81%
Gambling parents	25%	73%
Non-gambling parents	12%	85%
Has played truant	45%	53%
Has taken drugs	33%	64%
Receives tabloid newspaper at home	24%	73%

% 0 20 40 60 80 100

Source: British Survey of Children, the National Lottery & Gambling 2008–09, © *Ipsos MORI*

Awareness of legal age limits

Children were asked to name the legal age limit for buying National Lottery tickets, buying cigarettes, buying alcohol, driving and placing a bet in a betting shop. Children were less likely to know the correct age limit for buying National Lottery tickets than any other activity asked about. Underage National Lottery players, and those identified as problem gamblers, were more likely than average to say they thought National Lottery tickets could legally be purchased by people under the age of 16. The findings suggest that work to promote the legal age limit for buying National Lottery tickets would be of value generally, and that this may also help to further limit rates of under-age gambling, as some under-age players are potentially unaware that they are too young to purchase tickets legally.

Perceptions of parent's views

Results across the survey indicate that parental influence and behaviour plays a key role in under-age participation in gambling but that parents may be less likely to discuss gambling with their children than other potentially risky behaviours. For example, those who said their parents gambled were also more likely to gamble themselves (25 per cent, compared with 12 per cent of those who said their parents do not gamble). However, when asked to indicate how their parents would feel about children engaging in a number of potentially risky behaviours – such as smoking, taking drugs, drinking and gambling – children were less likely to know how their parents would feel about gambling on the National Lottery or fruit machines than other behaviours (23 per cent and 20 per cent respectively did not know what their parents would think, compared with five per cent who were unaware of their parents' views on cigarettes).

Asian children were no more likely than white and black children to gamble but Asian children who gambled were more likely to be problem gamblers

Free practice online gambling games

Despite high levels of Internet use among children, relatively small numbers (one per cent) had gambled with money online in the seven days preceding their interview. However, there is a strong relationship between playing free trial games online and 'offline' gambling. Regression

IPSOS MORI

analysis carried out by researchers at the University of Salford – which identified child characteristics that were associated with an increased probability of a child being a gambler or a problem gambler – revealed that playing free online gambling games in the past seven days was the single most important predictor of whether a child had gambled for money in the seven days preceding their interview, and one of the most important predictors of problem gambling among those who had gambled. The very high correlations might be interpreted as suggesting that it is not only the thrill of winning and losing money that makes a child gamble: those who are drawn to 'real' gambling are also attracted to 'pretend' gambling. The findings underline the importance of further research to investigate the relationship between playing trial games and real gambling, and the potential risks involved in children being able to access free trial games.

Characteristics of young gamblers

There were some interesting differences in gambling behaviours by ethnic group which may warrant further research. The regression analysis showed that Asian children were no more likely than white and black children to gamble but Asian children who gambled were more likely to be problem gamblers.

The regression modelling showed that where children live has a limited effect on their gambling behaviours: broadly, child gambling and problem gambling patterns were similar for children with similar characteristics attending similar types of school, irrespective of region.

Rates of gambling among children (on any type of game) are falling and, in line with this, the proportion of children classified as 'problem gamblers' has also fallen significantly over the past ten years

Statistical analysis identified a number of characteristics which are associated with significantly higher probabilities of children becoming gamblers and, among under-age gamblers, higher probabilities of displaying problem gambling behaviours. The regression models had a high degree of explanatory power, and could potentially be useful in targeting groups of children most at risk of developing problem gambling behaviours; for example, children attending schools where high proportions of the school roll are eligible for free school meals are more likely than those children attending schools where no pupils are eligible for free school meals to become problem gamblers, if they are gamblers.

Past-week spending on National Lottery tickets

Spending	%
Less than £1	5%
£1.00	33%
£1.01–£2.00	25%
£2.01–£3.00	16%
£3.01–£4.00	4%
£4.01–£5.00	9%
£5.01 or more	8%

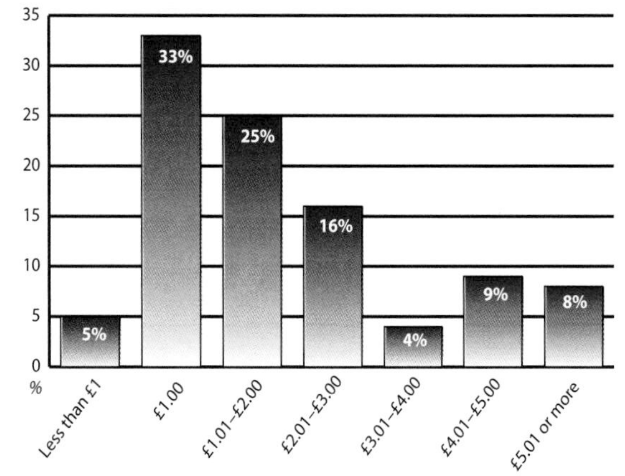

Location of ticket and scratchcard purchases

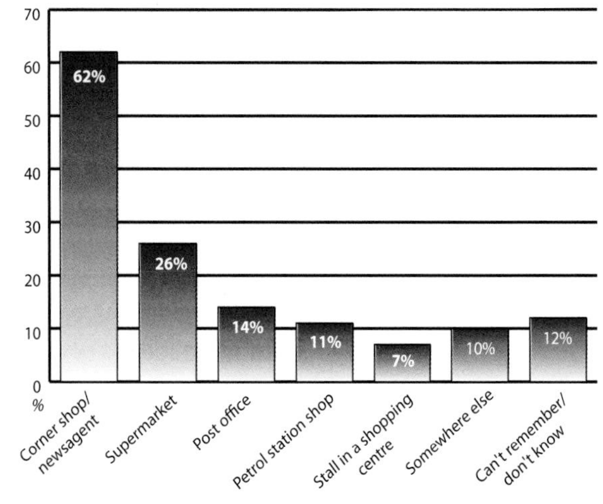

Location	%
Corner shop/newsagent	62%
Supermarket	26%
Post office	14%
Petrol station shop	11%
Stall in a shopping centre	7%
Somewhere else	10%
Can't remember/don't know	12%

Source: British Survey of Children, the National Lottery & Gambling 2008–09, © *Ipsos MORI*

Conclusions

The National Lottery Commission has commissioned several surveys to examine rates of child gambling in the past decade; the overall trends in youth participation revealed in these studies are encouraging. Not only are rates of seven-day gambling on the National Lottery on the decline but smaller proportions of children are attempting to buy National Lottery tickets and Scratchcards. More generally, rates of gambling among children (on any type of game) are falling and, in line with this, the proportion of children classified as 'problem gamblers' has also fallen significantly over the past ten years.

July 2009

⇨ The above information is an extract from Ipsos MORI's report *British Survey of Children, the National Lottery and Gambling 2008–09*, and is reprinted with permission. Please visit www.ipsos-mori.com for more.

IPSOS MORI

Young people and problem gambling

Information from GamCare.

Problem gambling doesn't just affect adults. There are an estimated 127,500 people aged under 24 with a gambling problem in the UK.

Factors linked with problem gambling in young people include:

- ⇨ Depression
- ⇨ Crime
- ⇨ Suicide
- ⇨ Anxiety
- ⇨ Low self-esteem
- ⇨ Personality disorders
- ⇨ Delinquent behaviour
- ⇨ Alcohol and substance abuse
- ⇨ Poor school performance and truancy

The most recent survey of young people and gambling was carried out in 2009 by Ipsos MORI for the National Lottery Commission. Nearly 9,000 adolescents aged between 12 and 15 were asked questions about their experiences of and attitudes towards gambling. The survey found that:

- ⇨ 21% had gambled in the past week.
- ⇨ 2% were estimated to have a gambling problem, which equates to around 60,000 people aged between 12 and 15. (The British Gambling Prevalence Survey also found that 0.9% of 16- to 24- year-olds had a gambling problem, which equates to 67,500 people.)
- ⇨ Boys were more likely to gamble and be problem gamblers than girls.
- ⇨ Asian children were no more likely to gamble than other ethnicities; however, they were more likely to be problem gamblers.

The number of young problem gamblers is likely to be even higher than that captured in prevalence research, as problem gambling has been labelled the 'hidden addiction'

The number of young problem gamblers is likely to be even higher than that captured in prevalence research, as problem gambling has been labelled the 'hidden addiction', with sufferers highly motivated to conceal their problem behaviour. And while this number may seem relatively small, it is important to remember that for every problem gambler, it has been estimated that a further eight people may be affected.

The rate of problem gambling is over three times as high in young people as it is in adults. However, it has consistently been shown that young people do not seek help for gambling problems. This may be due to a lack of awareness about problem gambling and avenues via which to seek help, but may also be due to the fact that many of those in positions of responsibility aren't alert to the problems excessive gambling can cause. Research has shown that only 5% of parents would take steps to encourage their child not to gamble.

There is a clear need for efforts to be made to educate young people, their families and those in positions of responsibility such as teachers and youth workers about problem gambling and how it can affect young people.

June 2010

⇨ The above information is reprinted with kind permission from GamCare. Please visit their website at www.gamcare.org.uk for more information on this and other related topics.

GAMCARE

Adolescent gambling on the Internet

A comprehensive overview of relevant literature on adolescent online gambling.

By Dr Mark Griffiths (Nottingham Trent University), Dr Jonathan Parke (Salford University), Dr Daniel King (University of Adelaide) and Dr Paul Delfabbro (University of Adelaide)

Some scene setting

- A national Internet gambling prevalence survey of 2,098 people in the UK by Griffiths (2001) included data from 119 adolescents (aged 15 to 19 years).
- No teenagers reported gambling on the Internet, but 4% of teenagers said they would like to try online gambling.
- Another study in Canada suggested at least a quarter of young people with serious gambling problems may be gambling on the Internet using 'free play' sites (for 'practice' and 'demonstration' purposes) (Hardoon, Derevensky & Gupta, 2002).

Empirical studies (prevalence)

- One in 12 young people aged 12 to 15 years (8%) said they had played a lottery game on the Internet in the past year. (Griffiths & Wood, 2007)
- 1% reported gambling on the Internet for money in the seven days prior to the survey. (Ipsos MORI, 2009)
- 8% had gambled on the Internet in the previous 12 months. (Brunelle, Gendron et al)
- 20% had gambled on the Internet, and just under 4% were regular Internet gamblers. (Olason et al, 2009a)
- 24% had gambled on the Internet, and just over 4% were regular Internet gamblers. (Olason et al, 2009b)
- They found that 2% of respondents reported gambling online in the past year. (Welte et al, 2009)
- Over the past year, almost one in 20 (4.6%) of the participants had gambled online with their own money. (Byrne, 2004)

Empirical studies (gender differences)

- Boys were more likely than girls to say they have played National Lottery games on the Internet (10% vs. 6%). (Griffiths & Wood, 2007)
- 13% males and 3% females had gambled on the Internet in the previous 12 months. (Brunelle, Gendron et al)
- Males were significantly more likely than females to gamble on the Internet (32% boys vs. 9% girls). (Olason et al, 2009b)
- Males were significantly more likely than females to gamble on the Internet (37% boys vs. 11.5% girls). (Olason et al, 2009b)
- 3% males and 0% females had gambled online in the 12 months preceding the interview. (Welte et al, 2009)
- Over the past year 7.8% males and 2.3% females had gambled online with their own money. When examined by age, those under 18 years were more likely to be male (8.6%; over 18 years 6.8%) than female (3.2%; over 18 years 1.3%). (Byrne, 2004)

Significantly more Internet gamblers (11%) were likely to be problem gamblers than those who did not gamble on the Internet (1.5%)

Empirical studies (problem gambling)

- 'Problem gamblers' were more likely than 'social gamblers' to have played a National Lottery game on the Internet (37% compared with 9%). (Griffiths & Wood, 2007)
- Significantly more Internet gamblers (11%) were likely to be problem gamblers than those who did not gamble on the Internet (1.5%). (Brunelle, Gendron et al)
- Prevalence of problem gambling among gamblers was 3%. However, among those who had gambled on the Internet, the problem gambling prevalence rates were significantly higher at 10.1%. (Olason et al, 2009)
- Prevalence of problem gambling among gamblers was 2.2%. However, among those who had gambled on the Internet, the problem gambling prevalence rate was 7.5%. (Olason et al, 2009)
- Internet gamblers were likely to experience more problem gambling symptoms by virtue of experimenting with more forms of gambling, as opposed to the properties of Internet gambling itself. (Welte et al, 2009)

NOTTINGHAM TRENT UNIVERSITY

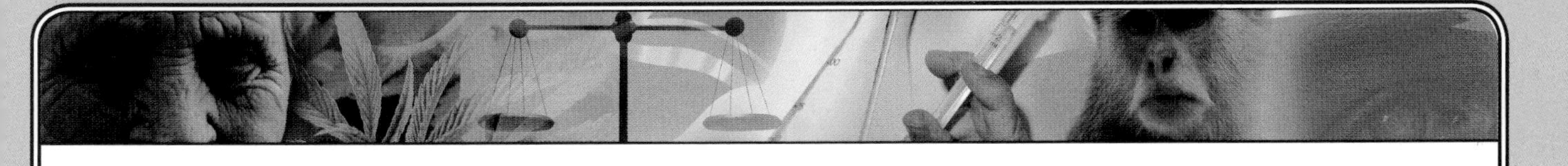

- For those who gambled on the Internet, the prevalence rate of problem gambling was almost 19%. (Byrne, 2004)

Online gambling-like experiences in adolescence

- North American studies have reported that anywhere between 25% to 50% of teenagers have played 'free play' games via Internet gambling sites (Derevensky & Gupta, 2007; McBride & Derevensky, 2009; Poulin & Elliot, 2007).
- Griffiths & Wood (2007) – Of the 8% who had gambled online, a quarter said they had played free instant win games (24%).
- Ipsos MORI (2009) – Just over a quarter of adolescents had played in 'money-free mode' in the week preceding the survey, with opportunities on the social networking sites four or five times more popular than those presented on real gambling sites.
- Brunelle et al – 35% of youth (49% males; 21% females) had played on the 'free play' / 'demo' mode on gambling sites.
- Byrne (2004) – More individuals under the age of 18 years than 18 to 24 years played 'free play' games on Internet gambling sites (43% vs. 33% for males; 42% vs. 29% for females).
- Forrest, McHale and Parke (2009) reported gambling in money-free mode was the single most important predictor of whether the child had gambled for money and important predictors of problem gambling. This relationship is correlational and not causal.
- The possibility and extent to which money-free gambling is responsible for real gambling participation and gambling-related risk and harm could only be confirmed using longitudinal data.
- It has been alleged that such opportunities encourage teenagers to practise before 'graduating' to playing for money games at online casinos (Kelley, Todosichuk, & Azmier, 2001).
- 'Precautionary principle' should be applied which prevents adolescents from being exposed to gambling-like experiences (Hyder & Juul, 2008).

Adolescent gambling via social networking sites

- Downs (2008) noted this activity has not been investigated, yet young people using these sites are able to gain access to gambling.
- Downs' pilot research – 25 poker applications on Bebo (and over 500 separate poker groups) and in excess of 100 poker applications on Facebook (and over 1,000 separate poker groups).
- Poker sites featured some with real prizes, some with cash-play options.
- All easily downloadable by children along with many free trial games.
- Largest of these poker groups had over several thousand members and in one group surveyed, 15% of those in the group declared they were under the age of 18 years.
- Furthermore, gambling applications typically contain sidebar advertisements and hyperlinks to real gambling sites.

Boys were more likely than girls to say they have played National Lottery games on the Internet (10% vs. 6%)

- Downs also reported a type of pseudo-gambling among 'Fluff Friends' that had over 100,000 active users per month.
- Users (typically young girls) create 'Fluff' Art to earn 'munny' (sic) – a type of virtual money through pet racing.
- Pet racing costs one point per race and winnings can be up to 4,000 points.
- Clearly there is no money changing hands but young children are learning the mechanics of gambling.
- Downs asserts there are serious questions about whether gambling with virtual money encourages positive attitudes towards gambling in young people.
- For instance, does gambling with virtual money lead to an increased prevalence of actual gambling?
- She also asks to what extent are gambling-related groups on social networking sites being used by those under 18 years and whether membership of such groups facilitates access to commercial gambling sites?
- It also seems only natural for youth to question whether they should game on Internet sites if they were winning 'play money'.

Discussion and conclusions

- Adolescents can and do gamble on the Internet.
- Adolescent Internet gamblers are significantly more likely than non-Internet gamblers to be problem gamblers.

NOTTINGHAM TRENT UNIVERSITY

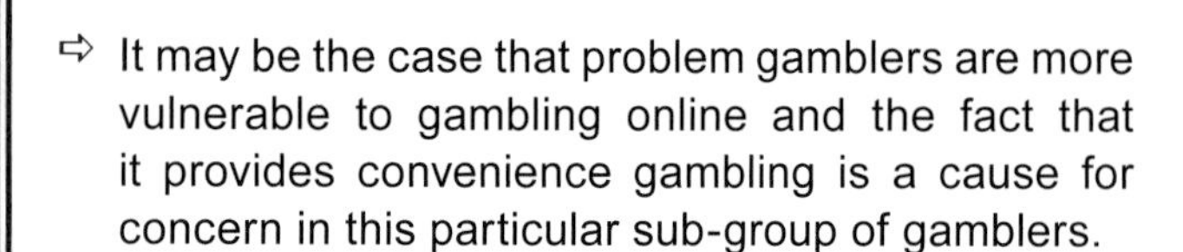

- It may be the case that problem gamblers are more vulnerable to gambling online and the fact that it provides convenience gambling is a cause for concern in this particular sub-group of gamblers.
- However, it may also be that adolescent problem gamblers gravitate to the Internet, adding it as an additional mode of gambling to their general repertoire of gambling behaviours.
- Given the paucity of the available evidence, the role of Internet gambling in creating adolescent problem gamblers should be treated with caution.
- However, it is clear that research which can help to identify the impact of Internet gambling on either creating or facilitating gambling-related harm among adolescents should be made a research priority.
- Such research should consider the potentially different roles that Internet gambling may play in creating new forms of harm and in exacerbating current forms of harm.

13% males and 3% females had gambled on the Internet in the previous 12 months

- Parents must have the appropriate attitudes, awareness and intentions to prevent under-age gambling.
- They may permit or assist their child as result of viewing such behaviour as a harmless and/or fun activity.
- Even if parents are motivated to prevent under-age Internet gambling, they must be prepared to monitor their child's behaviour.
- Where made available, spending on credit and debit cards and other forms of account should be monitored.
- Educating parents should be one of the key components of any strategy aimed at preventing/ minimising under-age Internet gambling.
- Finally, there is evidence to suggest that 'money free' gambling plays an important role for adolescents in conceptualising and experiencing Internet gambling.
- Approximately one-quarter to a third of adolescents have been reported to gamble in money-free mode.
- Ipsos MORI (2009) reported that 28% of 11- to 15-year-olds in a UK sample had done so within the last week.
- It is through money-free gambling (using social networking sites or 'demo' modes of real gambling sites) that children are being introduced to the principles and excitement of gambling without experiencing the consequences of losing money.
- Based on the available literature, it may be important to distinguish between the different types of money-free gambling being made available – namely social networking modes and 'demo' or 'free play' modes.
- Initial considerations suggest that these may be different both in nature and in impact.
- For example, as Downs (2008) argues, players gambling in social networking modes may experience a different type and level of reinforcement than those gambling in 'demo' mode.
- On some social networking sites the accumulation of 'play money' or 'points' may have implications for buying virtual goods or services or being eligible for certain privileges. This may increase the value and meaning of the gambling event to the individual.
- Individuals accessing money-free gambling through social networking sites may be more likely to be induced or persuaded to play given that these website visitors' primary intention may have been social interaction (i.e. the primary function of the website).
- This is different to those playing in 'demo' mode where gambling is the primary function of the website.
- Four or five times more children appear to report money-free gambling on social networking sites compared to 'demo' or 'free play' modes on gambling websites.
- The nature and impact of various forms of money-free gambling should be the subject of further research and empirical investigation.

Other potential concerns

Finally, it is worth noting there are other convergent gambling-like technologies that adolescents appear to be engaging in.

- The convergence of online gambling and video gaming.
- Online penny auctions.
- Television phone competitions via premium rate telephone lines.

22 September 2010

- The above information is reprinted with kind permission from Nottingham Trent University. Visit their website at www.ntu.ac.uk for more.

NOTTINGHAM TRENT UNIVERSITY

FAQ: problem gamblers

Information from National Council on Problem Gambling.

What is problem gambling?

Problem gambling includes all gambling behaviour patterns that compromise, disrupt or damage personal, family or vocational pursuits. The essential features are increasing preoccupation with gambling, a need to bet more money more frequently, restlessness or irritability when attempting to stop, 'chasing' losses, and loss of control manifested by continuation of the gambling behaviour in spite of mounting, serious, negative consequences. In extreme cases, problem gambling can result in financial ruin, legal problems, loss of career and family or even suicide.

Isn't problem gambling just a financial problem?

No. Problem gambling is an emotional problem that has financial consequences. If you pay all of a problem gambler's debts, the person will still be a problem gambler. The real problem is that they have an uncontrollable obsession with gambling.

Isn't problem gambling really the result of irresponsible or weak-willed people?

No. Many people who develop problems have been viewed as responsible and strong by those who care about them. Precipitating factors often lead to a change in behaviour, such as retirement or job-related stress.

What kind of people become problem gamblers?

Anyone who gambles can develop problems if they are not aware of the risks and do not gamble responsibly. When gambling behaviour interferes with finances, relationships and the workplace, a serious problem already exists.

Do casinos, lotteries and other types of gambling 'cause' problem gambling?

The cause of a gambling problem is the individual's inability to control the gambling. This may be due in part to a person's genetic tendency to develop addiction, their ability to cope with normal life stress and even their social upbringing and moral attitudes towards gambling. The casino or lottery provides the opportunity for the person to gamble. It does not, in and of itself, create the problem any more than a liquor store would create an alcoholic.

What types of gambling cause the most problem gambling?

Again, the cause of a gambling problem is the individual's inability to control the gambling. Therefore, any type of gambling can become problematic, just as an alcoholic can get drunk on any type of alcohol. But some types of gambling have different characteristics that may

NATIONAL COUNCIL ON PROBLEM GAMBLING

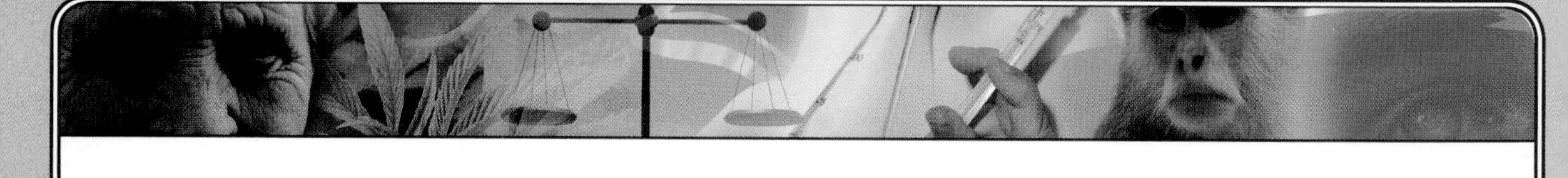

exacerbate gambling problems. While these factors are still poorly understood, anecdotal reports indicate that one risk factor may be a fast speed of play. In other words, the faster the wager to response time with a game, the more likely players may be to develop problems with a particular game.

What is the responsibility of the gaming industry?

Everyone who provides gambling opportunities has a responsibility to develop policies and programmes to address underage and problem gambling issues.

Can you be a problem gambler if you don't gamble every day?

The frequency of a person's gambling does not determine whether or not they have a gambling problem. Even though the problem gambler may only go on periodic gambling binges, the emotional and financial consequences will still be evident in the gambler's life, including the effects on the family.

just as tolerance develops to drugs or alcohol, the gambler finds that it takes more and more of the gambling experience to achieve the same emotional effect as before

How much money do you have to lose before gambling becomes a problem?

The amount of money lost or won does not determine when gambling becomes a problem. Gambling becomes a problem when it causes a negative impact on any area of the individual's life.

How can a person be addicted to something that isn't a substance?

Although no substance is ingested, the problem gambler gets the same effect from gambling as someone else might get from taking a tranquiliser or having a drink. The gambling alters the person's mood and the gambler keeps repeating the behaviour attempting to achieve that same effect. But just as tolerance develops to drugs or alcohol, the gambler finds that it takes more and more of the gambling experience to achieve the same emotional effect as before. This creates an increased craving for the activity and the gambler finds they have less and less ability to resist as the craving grows in intensity and frequency.

Are problem gamblers usually addicted to other things too?

It is generally accepted that people with one addiction are more at risk to develop another. Some problem gamblers also find they have a problem with alcohol or drugs. This does not, however, mean that if you have a gambling problem you are guaranteed to become addicted to other things. Some problem gamblers never experience any other addiction because no other substance or activity gives them the same feeling as the gambling does. There also appears to be evidence of family patterns regarding dependency, as many problem gamblers report one or both parents had a drinking and/or gambling problem.

⇨ The above information is reprinted with kind permission from the US-based National Council on Problem Gambling. Please visit their website at www.ncpgambling.org for more information on this and other related topics.

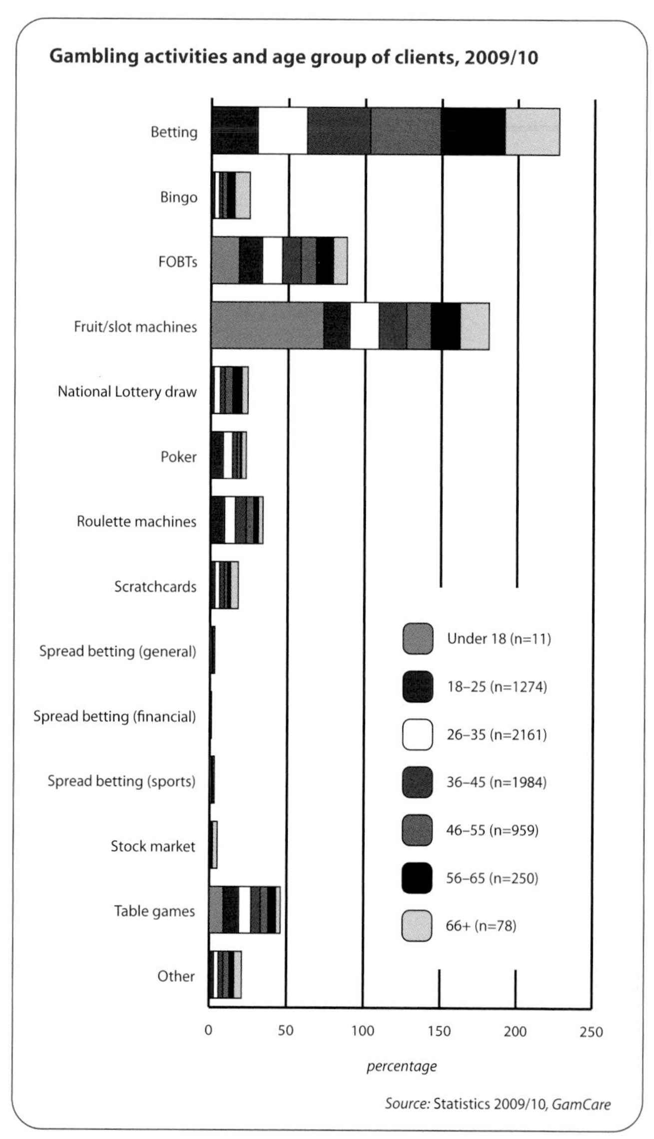

Problem gambling – 'the hidden addiction'

Information from Counselling Directory.

By Martina Blake, BSc Hons, MBACP

People from all walks of life can and do develop a problem with gambling – young people and children, teenagers, adults, retired people, professional people including those who work in the City, sportsmen and women, as well as those who work in the gambling industry.

UK research shows that a very small percentage of people who gamble recreationally go on to develop a problem or are adversely affected by it. This is still, however, hundreds of thousands of people in the UK with a problem, with very little specialist help provision compared to other dependencies.

Many who work in the field of treatment do feel, though, that there is a very big problem here because of the stigma in admitting to gambling problems. For example, the label of 'untrustworthy' comes with the territory, or the image perhaps of someone 'shifty' or 'dodgy' or the notion of being weak-willed. In addition, because it is not easily detected like heavy use of alcohol or drugs, for example, it tends to lend itself to going underground – often with a great suppression of emotions.

Problem gambling is simply more able to be hidden and can become protracted for great periods, leaving family members in great shock when the extent of the problem materialises, often years later. There may well be a lot of people who do not admit to having a problem at all because they are in denial, even to themselves. It is just too painful to acknowledge the deceit and the lies and many are hoping for that big win to redress the losses and make it all ok somehow. Given the proliferation in gambling forms and opportunities in recent years, there may well be a great many more people who have developed a gambling dependency than the figures suggest.

Help is available through some specialist providers, such as a national helpline (GamCare) which also has some counselling partners around the UK offering free counselling. There's residential rehab with the Gordon Moody Association, and in London, the Soho Problem Gambling Clinic. There's also the network of Gamblers Anonymous groups. For those with some financial means there are also private clinics, which provide help with a variety of dependencies and other problems. Private counselling and psychotherapy are other options.

It is certainly possible to tackle this dependency. If people are struggling then it can be valuable and very helpful to have some therapeutic input to examine this, raise self-awareness and begin a process of real dialogue, support and healing. In describing a problem gambler's life and experiences we look, as we go along, at anything that for them may have contributed to the problem or seems to be significant in some way. Examples might include: an early big win; a need to escape from some sort of trauma experienced; using as an escapism from stress; a parent or other significant person who gambled (or had other dependencies) in the family; being used to put on bets for other family members; going to the greyhound track with Dad as a special treat; going to bingo with Mum; an early introduction to gambling as a child; the importance of winning and losing in the family.

UK research shows that a very small percentage of people who gamble recreationally go on to develop a problem

There are so many individual and unique factors. These may not affect everyone in the same way because, for some, gambling stays recreational. Many go on to have no problem, but we do know that for some people it can set up something that is quite difficult to shift. For some we could perhaps say it is 'too' good at answering their needs and then it is difficult to stop because people are now 'needing' it rather than 'buying' a service or using it for recreation.

Gambling may start off as great fun, for some becoming a good companion or friend, with people identifying very strongly sometimes with it. Gambling can be quite useful in terms of answering a whole array of needs where these needs are not being met elsewhere, literally filling a void (the existential aspect). Of course it's something to do, a pastime: some may consider it as an easy way to make money (people are more inclined to remember the wins and suppress the losses), or get hooked on the 'high' of winning; for some it may be a lovely place to go, or be very convenient, fun and exciting in an otherwise humdrum existence.

In addition to exploring the personal history of, relationship with and forms of gambling (these may or may not vary over time) and any other dependencies or problems, an examination of the upside and adverse effects of the gambling needs to be undertaken – how is it problematic? This is usually so much more than just financial. Is too much time spent gambling; are crimes committed because of needing to fund it? Has it affected work, health, relationships; excluding other people, interests and opportunities? Not to forget the parts of life

that never were – problem gamblers speak about not having a home, car, children, holidays, relationships, the savings lost. There is often a huge sense of loss, very strong feelings of anger, frustration, sadness, shame and guilt. Depression and negative thinking enter the frame.

Boundaries typically start to go all over the place as people feel more desperate or cornered and the stakes get higher and higher, with gambling to get out of debt worsening the situation considerably. Relationships, for example, can be very badly affected. Problem gamblers often run from one situation to another, with strong repeating patterns. What it does to the person cannot be underestimated – the ups, the downs, the rollercoaster existence, exhaustion, real despair and despondency (it is not unusual for problem gamblers to feel suicidal and to attempt suicide). Family members may bail out the gambler time after time until in many cases the ties are broken. Family members suffer hugely also, which is why many of the specialist providers see these people too.

It is important to explore how a problem gambler might cope with day-to-day pressures and stressful events that may come up in life from time to time – what if there's a big disappointment, financial pressure, a bereavement, health issues? It is important to acknowledge that lapses are a part of recovery and to normalise these and look at strategies for coping and support systems in place. Some CBT work can be very effective in looking at the detail of a lapse (recording the actions, thoughts, feelings, physiology) – what do we make of it, what can we learn from it, where are the pivotal moments?

Very importantly, we look at how to create or make a different sort of life, and future hopes, dreams and goals. Creative work later in the process can be very powerful and provide a rich source of material for us, allowing more links and subtle nuances to emerge and facilitating bringing our work towards an end. Clients often enjoy this work and find something close to the heart here, something that really speaks to them.

For information and help on gambling addictions please visit www.martinablake.com

28 May 2010

⇨ The above information is reprinted with kind permission from Counselling Directory. Visit www.counselling-directory.org.uk for more information on this and other related topics.

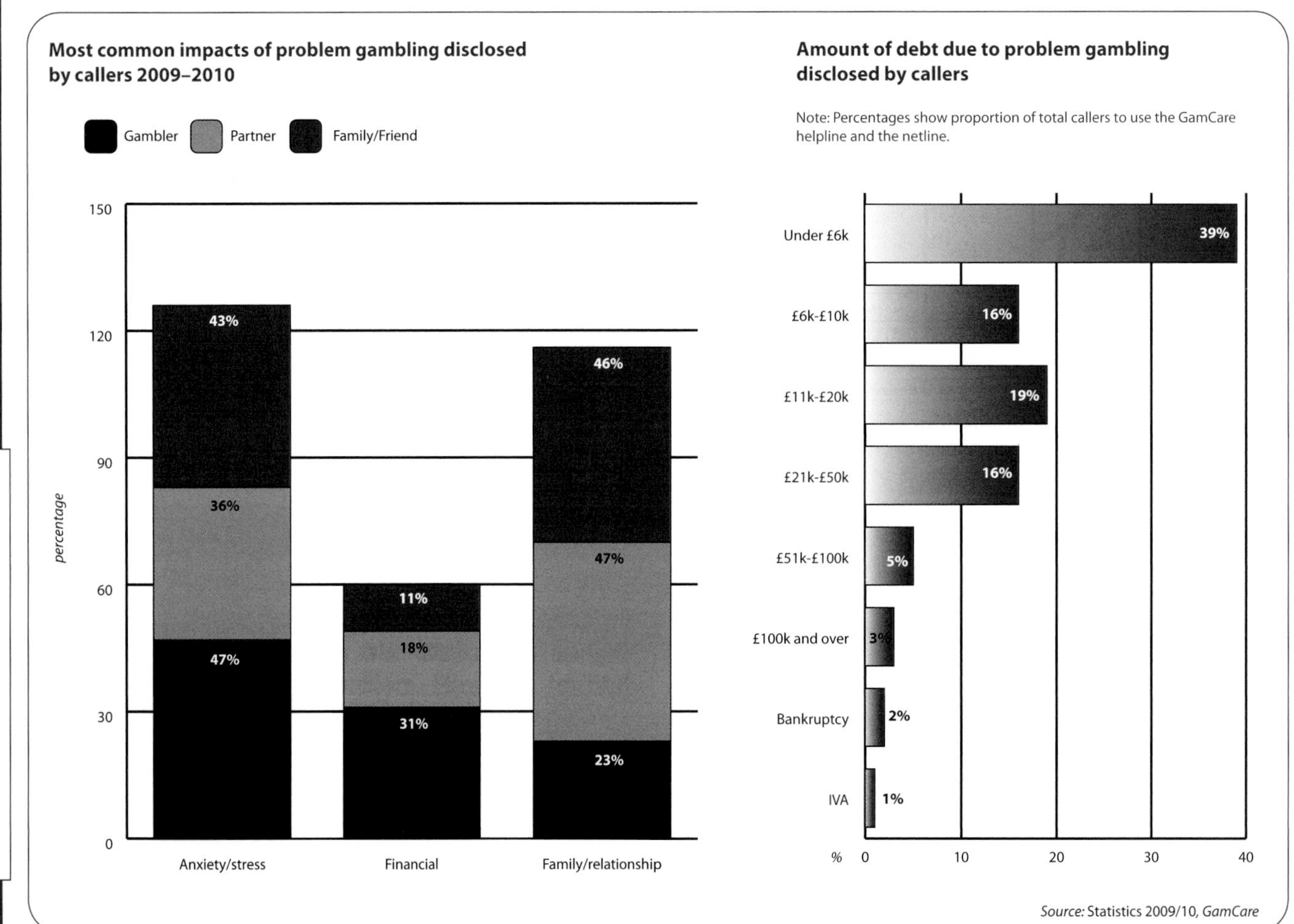

Problem gambling

Information from the Royal College of Psychiatrists.

How common is problem gambling?

Many of us like to place the odd bet or play the lottery, but it's only a problem for about six people in every 1,000.

Who is most likely to get this problem?

Across the world it seems to be common:

- in men – but this might just be because women gamble less than men;
- in teenagers and young adults – but problems of this sort can start at any age. Children as young as seven may find it difficult to control the amount of time they spend on computer games. Older people may have too much time on their hands;
- if someone else in your family – particularly one of your parents – is a problem gambler. This may be partly due to genes but can be learnt by seeing a parent gamble or being taught to gamble by them;
- in people who work in casinos, betting shops or amusement arcades;
- in certain types of gambling:
  - Internet gambling
  - Video poker
  - Dice games
  - Playing sports for money
  - High-risk stocks
  - Roulette;
- if you drink heavily or use illegal drugs;
- if you have depression, anxiety or bipolar affective disorder (manic depression).

Is it a problem for me?

Answer 'yes' or 'no' to each of these ten questions:

- Do I spend a lot of time thinking about gambling?
- Am I spending larger amounts of money on my gambling?
- Have I tried to cut down or stop gambling but not been able to?
- Do I get restless or irritable if I try to cut down my gambling?
- Do I gamble to escape from life's difficulties or to cheer myself up?
- Do I carry on playing after losing money to try and win it back?
- Have I lied to other people about how much time or money I spend gambling?
- Have I ever stolen money to fund my gambling?
- Has my gambling affected my relationships or my job?
- Do I get other people to lend me money when I have lost?

If you have answered 'yes':

- Just once – may be a problem. This one thing may be enough of a problem to need help.
- Three times – problem gambling. Your gambling probably feels out of control – think about getting help.
- Five or more times – pathological gambling. Your gambling is probably affecting every part of your life – get help.

Across the world [problem gambling] seems to be common in men – but this might just be because women gamble less than men

How do you lose control of your gambling?

You may gamble:

- to forget about responsibilities;
- to feel better when you feel depressed or sad;
- to fill your time when bored (especially if not working);
- when you drink or use drugs;
- when you get angry with others – or yourself.

Or, you may have:

- started gambling early – some people start as young as seven or eight;
- never been able to control your gambling;
- one or both parents who are problem gamblers.

ROYAL COLLEGE OF PSYCHIATRISTS

Should I stop gambling or try to control it?

The first thing is to decide to get help – you can then work out whether you are ready to stop or just want to control your gambling better. Many people just want to control their gambling, but then decide to stop completely.

Living with a problem gambler

- Being married to or a partner of a problem gambler, or being their parent or child, is hard and can be distressing.
- Your loved one will probably have tried to hide the size of the problem from you, while they have at the same time borrowed or stolen to pay off debts.
- If, with the help of the ten questions above, you can see that gambling is a problem for someone in your family, it's best to be honest with him or her about it. They need to know about the pain and trouble they are causing other people and that help is there for them.
- If your gambling relative doesn't take any notice, you can get support for yourself from one of the services listed on page 25. There are groups and individual sessions to support family members.

Being married to or a partner of a problem gambler, or being their parent or child, is hard and can be distressing. Your loved one will probably have tried to hide the problem

ROYAL COLLEGE OF PSYCHIATRISTS

The risks

Problem gamblers are more likely than other people to:

- become depressed;
- have alcohol or drug problems;
- commit suicide out of desperation because of their feelings of being trapped by their debts;
- be separated or divorced;
- have committed a crime to support their gambling.

It's better to get help before you run into trouble.

Where can I get help?

All of the following provide free support to help you cut down or stop gambling:

- NHS: The CNWL National Problem Gambling Clinic in London has doctors, nurses, therapists, psychologists, debt counsellors and family therapists with special experience in helping problem gamblers.
- GamCare – runs the national HelpLine and its online equivalent, the NetLine, to offer help and support for people with a gambling problem, their family and friends. GamCare also provides face-to-face online counselling in many parts of the UK.
- The Gorden Association – a charity which provides treatment and housing for problem gamblers.
- The 12-step meetings of Gamblers Anonymous.
- Gamanon: groups for relatives of problem gamblers.

What sort of help is there?

Cognitive Behavioural Therapy (CBT)

Research has shown that CBT can:

- reduce the number of days a person gambles;
- reduce the amount of money they lose;
- help a gambler to stay away from gambling once they have stopped.

How does CBT work? If you are a problem gambler, you will think differently from other people about your betting. You will tend to believe that:

- you are more likely to win than you would expect by chance;
- in a game with random numbers, like roulette, certain numbers are more likely to come up than others;
- winning twice in a row means that you are on a 'winning streak' – so you bet larger and larger sums;
- you are more likely to win at a game of chance if you are familiar with it;
- certain rituals can bring you luck;
- having lost, you can somehow win back your losses by gambling more.

CBT is given in around ten one-hour sessions. The sessions focus on these ways of thinking, but also on how you feel and behave when you want to bet or when you are gambling. CBT helps you to work out more helpful ways of thinking and behaving. A diary helps you to keep track of your improvement. In the months following treatment, follow-up CBT sessions in a group seem to help people stay away from gambling longer.

How does CBT compare with other treatments? We don't know yet – there have not been enough large studies to be clear about this.

12-step programmes

This is an approach which assumes that a dependence on drink or gambling is a disease and that the best

people to support you are those who have had similar experiences. Regular meetings are held in which people can share the problems they have had and the ways in which they have overcome them. They also have a 'buddy' system, where each member has another member whom they can contact if they feel that they are about to drink or gamble again. The 12-step fellowship, Gamblers Anonymous, offers meetings throughout the UK and many problem gamblers find these meetings helpful. You may also need practical help:

- Managing your debts;
- Dealing with family problems;
- Treating other psychological/psychiatric problems, e.g. depression.

CBT can reduce the number of days a person gambles, reduce the amount of money they lose and help a gambler to stay away from gambling once they have stopped

Medication

No medication is licensed for the treatment of problem gambling in the UK but antidepressants can be prescribed to help with low moods.

What if I don't get help?

About a third of problem gamblers will recover on their own without treatment and about two in three will continue to have problems, which tend to get worse.

How to get help and when

Don't wait until life does not seem worth living. If you get help, you will feel better and avoid many problems with your life and health.

No medication is licensed for the treatment of problem gambling in the UK but antidepressants can be prescribed to help with low moods

You can refer yourself by calling or emailing the contacts below:

- NHS: CNWL National Problem Gambling Clinic: 1 Frith Street, London W1D 3HZ, Tel: 020 7534 6699; email: gambling.cnwl@nhs.net
- GamCare: Helpline 0845 6000 133
- Gordon Moody Association: Tel: 01384 241 292
- GA (Gamblers Anonymous): Tel: 020 7384 3040
- GAM-ANON UK and Ireland: Tel: 08700 50 8880.

For references please see original text at: http://www.rcpsych.ac.uk/mentalhealthinfoforall/problems/problemgambling.aspx

June 2010

- The above information is reprinted with kind permission from the Royal College of Psychiatrists. Please visit www.rcpsych.ac.uk for more information on this and other related topics.

ROYAL COLLEGE OF PSYCHIATRISTS

Britain's binge-gambling problem

The number of compulsive gamblers has exploded as feared, but money spent on treatment and awareness is still lacking.

Experts' fears of an explosion in the number of compulsive gamblers in the UK have proved prophetic, with 600,000 Britons now reckoned to have a gambling problem, compared with less than half that figure in 2004. Despite the marked increase in addiction and continued calls for regulation, evidence suggests little is being done to stamp out the aggressive marketing and deceptive practices of gaming providers.

As with the tobacco and alcohol industries, successive governments have proved loath to significantly rein in the gambling world for fear of the impact on the nation's tax coffers. At the same time, the advent of online gaming has fragmented the industry, with the mass of offshore and laxly-regulated casino and betting sites proving far harder to control than traditional high-street bookmakers and bingo halls. Last week's banning of Prime Scratchcards' 'irresponsible' online promotion was a small success for those calling for tighter regulation, but in the wider scheme of things barely scratched the surface of the problem with the industry's marketing tactics.

Prime Scratchcards used testimony from a lucky punter to suggest that online gambling could be a solution to financial problems:

'I am a single mom and I live on family benefits, I played and won £46,799 and it is incredible for me. I was very stressed for my son's future and I couldn't sleep, now that I won I know that I can help my son build a better future.'

Women in particular have become a prime target of gaming companies in recent years. Thanks to their relatively late entry into the betting arena compared with their male counterparts, the female market is considered a major area of growth for gambling operators. According to compulsive-gambler-turned-author Marilyn Lancelot, 'Ten years ago there were a handful of women gambling... That has changed with more women earning an income, raising families without a spouse, freedom to enter gambling establishments without an escort, and thus creating more female gamblers.'

The specific targeting of women is just one example of the net being cast ever wider by gambling operators desperate to increase revenues and profits. Thanks to the proliferation of online betting companies, margins are becoming tighter and competition for new business progressively more fierce. As a result, operators are taking extreme measures to attract customers, hurling bonuses and free bets around with abandon, safe in the knowledge that the house will always win in the end.

A study by the University of Illinois concluded that the introduction of gambling to a certain area increased the number of problem gamblers by anywhere between 100% and 550%; because of the unparalleled penetration of Internet casinos and bookmakers compared with their offline peers, the potential for catastrophe is far higher than ever before. Reports routinely surface of new pockets of problem gambling throughout the country, yet the best that the combined forces of the gambling industry and the Government can come up with is an annual 'Responsible Gambling Awareness Day' and vague, unfulfilled promises not to make gambling accessible to a vulnerable audience.

At the very least, gaming companies ought to be spending more on treating those who have developed crippling gambling problems as a result of their exposure to the industry. The British Medical Association has called on gambling operators to raise their collective contributions to treatment programmes from the £3.6m paid in 2007 to at least £10m – a figure which would still only amount to less than £17 per problem gambler. The government, meanwhile, collects annual tax revenues of around £2bn from gambling, indicating the scale of Britain's continued love affair with betting in all its guises.

Despite the inherent dangers and dubious ethics of gambling, the betting industry's image continues to be softened in the eyes of potential punters. Whereas alcohol and tobacco advertising has long been subject to stringent restrictions in the realm of sport and elsewhere, casino companies' logos are still sported proudly on some of Britain's most prominent football teams. At the same time, the media plays a vital part in promoting gambling as part of the national furniture. Most newspapers hand out betting advice in their sports pages, while their websites offer direct links to betting companies alongside news of upcoming fixtures.

Just because gambling is justified by some as a benign leisure activity does not automatically make it a safe and sedate product to be promoted at every opportunity, and those regulating the industry should show far more concern for the darker side of gambling. More and more impressionable people – both young and old – are being targeted by gaming companies

THE GUARDIAN

every year, yet spending on the treatment of addiction and warning of the dangers of gambling has not even come close to keeping pace.

Such a disparity is a recipe for disaster, and unless the issue is taken in hand, compulsive betting will become an even greater menace than it is at present, presenting Britain with a binge-gambling problem to rival its binge-drinking culture.

3 February 2010

Drug treatments for adolescents with gambling problems?

A new review article from the principal investigators of the NCRG Centers of Excellence in Gambling Research at Yale University and the University of Minnesota explores the potential of pharmacological treatments for disordered gambling in adolescents.

It is important to identify an effective treatment for this age group, as adolescents are at a higher risk for developing gambling-related problems than adults. However, no drug trials focused on pathological gambling have been conducted with this age group. Determining which drugs might be safe, tolerable and effective for adolescents is more complex than simply applying what we already know about pharmacological treatments for adults (Grant & Potenza, 2010).

Currently, there are no pharmacological treatments approved by the US Food and Drug Administration (FDA) for pathological gambling, though several drugs have shown potential in this area. One medication that has performed well in clinical trials is naltrexone, which has been used to blunt cravings for alcohol. Several studies suggest that naltrexone can reduce the intensity of gambling urges among adults with pathological gambling. Naltrexone is currently approved by the FDA as a treatment for alcohol dependence, and has been used in small doses to treat adolescents.

Lithium, currently used to treat bipolar disorder, is another medication with potential. It has been shown to reduce thoughts and urges associated with pathological gambling in people with both bipolar spectrum disorders and pathological gambling. One attribute that makes lithium particularly appealing is that it has been used safely with adolescents to treat bipolar disorder.

According to the authors, it is difficult to translate pharmacological treatments to adolescents because the adolescent brain is 'a changing organ' (Grant & Potenza, 2010, p129). That is, the brain's developmental processes may cause a drug to affect adolescents differently than adults depending on their individual stage of maturation. Consequently, research on adults can only suggest potentially promising pharmacological treatments. Definitive treatment recommendations for adolescents will have to wait for the completion of clinical trials in this population that include a control group for comparison.

References

Grant, J. E., & Potenza, M. N. (2010). Pharmacological treatment of adolescent pathological gambling. *International Journal of Adolescent Medicine and Health*, 22(1), 129-138.

⇨ The above information is reprinted with kind permission from the US-based National Center for Responsible Gaming. Visit www.gamblingdisorders.org for more information.

Internet poker ruined my life

When Jane started lying to her husband to hide the thousands of pounds of debt she was in, she knew her addiction to Internet poker was out of control. Now 24 and pregnant, she talks about how her addiction is threatening her future.

By Marcella Carnevale

Money worries

I started playing Internet poker three years ago when I moved to London. I was unemployed, trying to find work and felt very secluded with a lot of time on my hands. My friends were gambling online so I thought I'd give it a try, but I quickly realised my gambling was out of control. My husband's a teacher and money was tight. Even though we only had £20 a week for food, I was spending £100 a day gambling on my credit card while he was at work. I knew it was wrong to beg him for money whilst spending so much on Internet poker, but I just couldn't stop.

'My friends were gambling online so I thought I'd give it a try, but I quickly realised my gambling was out of control'

I finally found a job but I was coming home and playing from 7pm until two in the morning. My husband would be watching television while I was sitting next to him gambling. If I'd had a busy or horrible day, gambling seemed like an easy way to switch off, except I'd end up more worked up than when I'd started.

Heavy losses

I've lost about £8,000 over three years, all on credit cards. I'm three months' pregnant and will soon be stopping work, but I'm still hoping for an elusive gambling win that will enable me to buy everything I want. It's really difficult for me to give up the idea that I'm going to get rich from gambling, rather than saving and clearing my debts. I'm dazzled by that golden pot of money. If I could just play three times a week I'd be happy, but I don't have the control. Now, I'm playing for three hours a night, which for me is quite restrained.

Trying to stop

Five months ago, I disconnected the Internet. It was the only way I could stop gambling and it was blissful. Not having the temptation there made me feel a lot happier.

I started again a month ago after getting pregnant. I had to give up cigarettes and alcohol, and since I often played drunk, I thought playing sober would help me control how much I was spending. I've tried to regulate the amount, keeping it to £50 a month, but I constantly slip up and find myself putting in another couple of hundred pounds. Unlike my other vices of drinking and smoking, gambling has had a lasting effect, leaving me significantly poorer, with a genuine debt problem.

THESITE.ORG

Lying to cover my tracks

My husband knows I've lost money but not how much. In an effort to curb my gambling, he set up my online gambling account so each time I deposit or withdraw money, he's notified via email. However, I know his password and to cover how much I'm spending, I've been deleting his emails. I recently deleted a series of emails from his inbox in the early hours of the morning, which showed I'd lost £600 in nine hours of solid gambling. He found out when he borrowed my cash cards to get some shopping and discovered there was no money on either, so he ended up confiscating them.

'I've lost about £8,000 over three years, all on credit cards...It's really difficult for me to give up the idea that I'm going to get rich from gambling, rather than saving and clearing my debts'

Terrible mood swings

It's not just losing money which has had a negative effect on my life. My gambling mood swings are awful. If I've just won a big hand, I'm in a good mood and really nice, but if I've had a bit of bad luck or played badly, I can be a real a******e to my husband. I take it out on him and go from being really happy to being really down, which is very unpleasant for him and puts a strain on our relationship.

My career and friendships have also suffered because of gambling. I'd stay up until three in the morning and then drag myself into work exhausted. For a while I worked from home, but I found myself playing poker instead of working. I was detached and couldn't concentrate. None of my friends' company is as good as gambling online.

Dangers of Internet gambling

With Internet gambling, you can just click a button and money is transferred into your account, but the money slips away really quickly. The world of live gambling is heavily regulated, but online anyone can gamble. I know of 15-year-olds who play on their dads' accounts. It's really easy to bet with money you can't see, and you can lose £1,000 in a night.

Breaking free

I know I have to stop and the only way is by disconnecting the Internet again. If someone is playing obsessively and can't afford to lose the amounts they're gambling with, they should try to stop and get help. I hope I can stop gambling and manage my money so I'm debt free before my baby arrives.

With Internet gambling, you can just click a button and money is transferred into your account, but the money slips away really quickly

➪ The above information is reprinted with kind permission from TheSite.org. Visit www.thesite.org for more information.

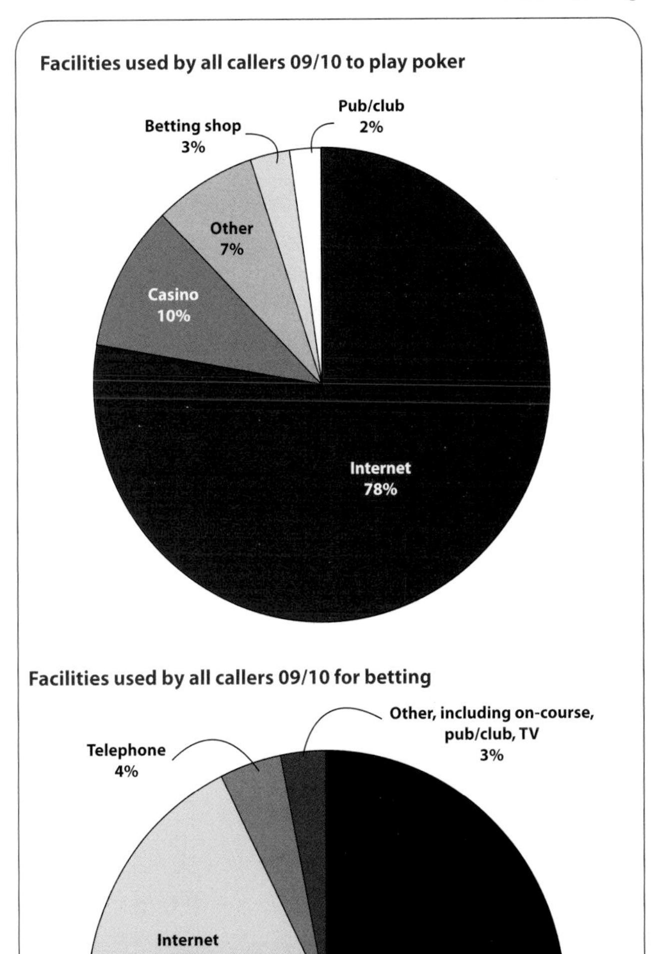

THESITE.ORG

Gambling addiction linked to genes

'Gambling addiction can be inherited,' the Daily Mail reported.

The newspaper said, 'if one of your parents is addicted to gambling the odds are high that you will be as well, research has revealed'.

This study in 2,889 pairs of twins investigated the role of genetic and environmental factors in the development of gambling addiction. The researchers were particularly interested in whether these factors interact in the same way in women's gambling addiction as in men's.

The study found that identical twins who were gamblers were more likely to have a twin who was also a gambler than non-identical twins. The researchers suggest that this association was more to do with a genetic link than environmental factors.

This study suggests there is a genetic component to gambling addiction that can be present in both men and women. However, this study did not address which genes may be involved or the strength of the association. Addictions are complex disorders. If some people do have a genetic predisposition to develop addictions, it is unlikely to be the sole cause of the addiction and environmental factors are also likely to be involved.

This study suggests there is a genetic component to gambling addiction that can be present in both men and women

Where did the story come from?

The study was carried out by researchers from the University of Missouri and the Queensland Institute of Medical Research. It was funded by the US National Institutes of Health. The study was published in the peer-reviewed medical journal *Archives of General Psychiatry.*

What kind of research was this?

The researchers say that women represent nearly half of all individuals who are in treatment for gambling addiction. They wanted to investigate the causes of this addiction in women and whether the causes differed to gambling addiction in men.

This was a cross-sectional twin study. Some previous studies have suggested that gambling addiction runs in families. Twin studies such as this are a good way to investigate whether genetic or environmental factors underlie a condition.

What did the research involve?

The study included 4,764 participants from a previous study called the Australian Twin Registry cohort II. Between 2004 and 2007, the cohort members were contacted by telephone and interviewed to assess their gambling behaviours.

The average age of the participants was 38, and 57% of the sample was female. There were 1,875 complete twin pairs, 867 of these pairs were monozygotic (identical), while the other 1,008 were dizygotic (non-identical). There were also 1,014 individual twins from incomplete twin pairs. Of these, 304 were individuals who had a monozygotic twin and 710 had a dizygotic twin. As monozygotic twins have identical genes, whereas dizygotic twins share only half the same genes, the researchers were able to assess the likelihood that correlations in traits between twins were inherited genetically.

Participants that reported gambling at least five times a year were given further psychiatric diagnostic criteria to assess whether they had a gambling problem. Most participants (77.5%) surpassed this five times a year threshold. The psychiatric evaluations were made using established criteria called DSM-IV. This allowed the researchers to assess how many of the ten DSM-IV symptoms of pathological gambling the participants had.

The researchers also screened the participants for mania, as a person experiencing a manic episode may be more likely to gamble. This ensured that people diagnosed as gambling addicts were not gambling as a consequence of mania or other mental health problems.

The researchers used data from a previous telephone interview, conducted between 1996 and 2000, to assess whether the twins shared a similar environment. Each twin had been asked how often they shared friends and dressed alike when they were between six and 13 years and whether they had been in the same class in primary and high school. The twins were also asked how often they saw or contacted each other so the researchers could assess how similar their adult environment was.

What were the basic results?

Many of the twins were frequent gamblers, but only 2.2% of the twins were classified as pathological gamblers. This was 3.4% of the men and 1.2% of the women.

NHS CHOICES

Monozygotic twins (both male and female) had a higher rate of both twins being pathological gamblers than dizygotic twins. The researchers calculated the likelihood (correlation) of both twins being gamblers, and gave it a score between 0 (no correlation) and 1 (strong correlation).

Male monozygotic twins had a correlation of 0.49 compared with 0.21 for male dizygotic twins. Female monozygotic twins had a correlation of 0.55 compared with 0.21 for female dizygotic twins.

The researchers estimated that participants who had one pathological gambling DSM-IV symptom had a 49% chance that it was inherited. Participants who had three or more symptoms had a 58% chance and those who had five or more symptoms (a clinical diagnosis of pathological gambling) had a 40% chance of it being inherited.

There was no association between twins who were both pathological gamblers and who had a shared environment, suggesting that environmental factors did not play a role.

How did the researchers interpret the results?

The researchers suggest that their study has established for the first time that genes are as important in the cause of disordered gambling in women as they are in men.

They say 'the discovery of specific genes and environments involved in the development of disordered gambling remains an important direction for future research'.

Conclusion

This relatively large study assessed whether there was an increased likelihood for a twin to have a gambling problem if their brother or sister did. The researchers suggest that gambling addiction was likely to be inherited and that this was due to genetic factors rather than twins growing up in a shared environment. However, there are a few limitations of their study that should be taken into account when interpreting the findings.

- The study looked at an Australian population. It is not known whether the results of this study can be generalised to other populations.
- While the study tried to separate environmental from inherited effects, it is still possible that these results were in part due to environmental factors. The researchers calculated to what extent each pair of twins had a shared environment while they were growing up by asking six broad questions. These questions may not have been able to distinguish all environmental factors that can affect a person's likelihood of developing a gambling problem. Additionally, the twins were asked to recall this information, and there may have been differences between the way individuals perceived or remembered their past. This may have been affected further by their knowledge of their own and their siblings' gambling habits.

There is no single reason why addictions develop. Use of substances such as alcohol, drugs and nicotine changes the way we feel, both mentally and physically. Some people enjoy this and feel a strong desire to repeat it. Activities such as gambling may cause a 'high' if you win, followed by a desire to repeat the success. Eventually, this grows into a habit that cannot be broken because it has become a regular part of life.

This is a preliminary study and further research is needed to understand the factors that trigger gambling addiction.

11 June 2010

- Reproduced by kind permission of the Department of Health.

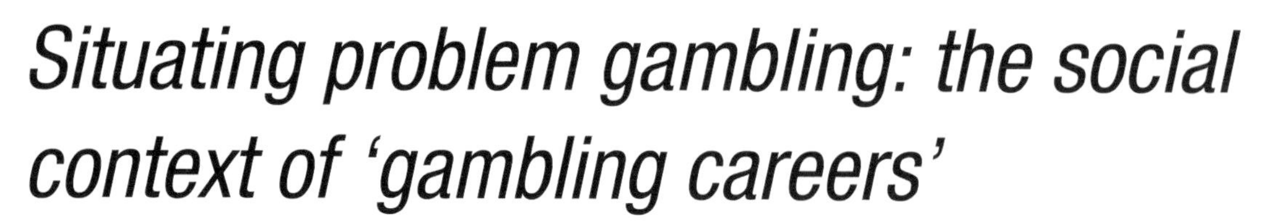

Situating problem gambling: the social context of 'gambling careers'

Research summary.

This three-year study is funded by the Economic and Social Research Council and the Responsibility in Gambling Trust. It is being conducted by Dr Gerda Reith, who is the Principal Investigator, at the University of Glasgow, and the Scottish Centre for Social Research (ScotCen): www.scotcen.org.uk

The research benefits from the input of two Advisory Groups: a national group that includes representatives from the fields of policy, voluntary organisations, treatment providers and gamblers' organisations, as well as an international group comprised of academic and research specialists in the field of gambling studies.

In addition, Dr Rachel Volberg, President of Gemini Research and Director of the US National Council on Problem Gambling, will be acting as specialist consultant to the research.

Summary of the research

In the past decade, increasing liberalisation has transformed the climate of gambling in Britain, bringing the activity to greater numbers of people than ever before and culminating in the Gambling Act of 2005, which recognised and regulated this shift. While most people enjoy their gambling, a significant minority experience problems, including poverty, debt, familial breakdown and personal hardship from behaviour that has become out of control.

Despite the increased popularity of the activity among large sections of the population however, surprisingly little is known about the actual motivations, characteristics and lifestyles of gamblers and problem gamblers themselves. This study attempts to fill this knowledge gap by developing a new conceptual framework for understanding the pathways through which individuals enter into and recover from problematic gambling behaviour in the notion of 'gambling careers'. It aims to situate both gambling and problem gambling behaviour in its social context in order to both explore how behaviour changes over the life course of individuals, and how it is influenced by local cultures and meanings.

It starts from the assumption that no-one is born a gambler, but rather that gambling is a complex social activity that is learned over time. Through in-depth interviews with particular groups of gamblers over a three-year period, the research will explore the motivations, attitudes and self-perceptions of gamblers and problem gamblers, drawing out the meanings that gambling has for them and how this influences behaviour in a series of rich narrative accounts.

Age, gender, class, ethnicity and even geography are all likely to influence the cultures of different groups of gamblers

It is recognised that different types of people play different types of games, and for very different reasons. There are significant differences between, for example, women playing afternoon bingo, wealthy high rollers playing high stakes games in casinos and Internet gamblers playing alone in their homes. Age, gender, class, ethnicity and even geography are all likely to influence the cultures of different groups of gamblers. At the same time, there may be similarities across all these types of behaviour, and it is this that this study will explore. It will contact individuals from casinos, betting shops, fruit machine arcades and bingo halls, as well as recruiting Internet and lottery gamblers, to analyse the similarities as well as the differences in behaviour.

The research will investigate a variety of experiences of gambling: the pathways through which individuals begin and continue gambling, enter problem behaviour and move out of it, and the relation of these stages to broader socio-demographic factors, attitudes and self-perceptions. The influence of families, friends and communities in shaping individuals' gambling careers, as well as the impacts gamblers' behaviour has on them, will also be explored.

UNIVERSITY OF GLASGOW

Rather than viewing problem gamblers as a relatively small and distinct group, the study will look at problematic behaviour as a particular phase that can affect many more individuals at some point(s) in a gambling career, and will examine the way that behaviour waxes and wanes among this larger group. It will focus on key moments and processes of change such as, for example, how people begin gambling, points when playing increases or decreases, when individuals realise they have a problem and decide to seek help – or not – and the circumstances that surround this.

Experiences of treatment, perceptions of its benefits, as well as relapses and reasons for leaving it, will also be explored. Given that the vast majority of problem gamblers never seek treatment, the research will focus in particular on the phase of 'natural recovery' in which problematic behaviour is resolved without formal intervention, and will explore shifts in social, demographic and personal circumstances that are associated with it.

This approach to gambling will allow the research to move beyond more static 'snapshots' of individuals, to investigate the fluid and dynamic processes involved in gambling behaviour, allowing an examination of the 'how' and 'why' of change over time.

The research summary above is from the University of Glasgow:www.glasgow.ac.uk

Key findings

This project aimed to provide a sociological account of the ways in which gambling develops and changes over time in what are termed 'gambling careers'. Its objective was to place problem gambling in its wider social context by focusing on how people begin gambling, move towards and away from problem gambling, and their experiences of recovery.

- ⇨ Almost all respondents had been introduced to gambling through their families.
- ⇨ Most had at least one close family member who gambled – many first-timers gambled with the support of a family network.
- ⇨ Gambling knowledge and behaviour was often embedded in the routines of daily family life. It was intergenerational and patterns of gambling were specific to male and female family members.
- ⇨ Women became aware of, and had their first experience of, gambling through female relatives – often bingo or slot machines.
- ⇨ Men were introduced to gambling through male relatives, which often took the form of sports betting.
- ⇨ Experiences of gambling tended to have begun between eight to 12 years of age, especially among those from lower socio-economic groups. Many went on to become problem gamblers in later life.
- ⇨ For those who began gambling for the first time later in life, friends and colleagues helped facilitate the gambling. This pattern was often associated with more affluent respondents, whose behaviour developed alongside patterns of employment, and the location of the workplace to opportunities for gambling. Gambling was also a reflection of an individual's socialising and friendships.
- ⇨ Acting as social hubs, bingo halls, betting shops, arcades and pubs were all found to play a crucial role in local communities, often forming an environment in which heavy drinking was common.
- ⇨ Changes in behaviour were common among the respondents. The majority were found to move into, and out of, periods of heavy gambling – even during the relatively short period of the study.
- ⇨ Four forms of gambling patterns were identified: reduction over time; increase over time; a fluctuating pattern; and no change. Factors causing changes were complex and interdependent, but often included changes in financial and life circumstances (e.g. bereavement, employment status, or end of a relationship).
- ⇨ For some players, gambling acted as a coping mechanism to escape from the daily stresses of life. For others, it was a source of excitement and sociability.
- ⇨ Reducing or recovering from problem gambling tended to be triggered by events involving family, 'rock bottom' experiences, 'maturing out' of playing, or having a change in self-perception.
- ⇨ Counselling services, self-help organisations and family support were often found to help the recovery process.

Note

Professor Gerda Reith of the Department of Sociology, Anthropology and Applied Social Science at the University of Glasgow and Simon Anderson of the Scottish Centre for Social Research, Edinburgh, carried out this project.

⇨ The above information is reprinted with kind permission from the Economic and Social Research Council. Visit www.esrcsocietytoday.ac.uk for more information.

Gamblers in debt need better education and joined-up help

Information from GamCare.

The research, the result of a ground-breaking collaboration between GamCare, the Money Advice Trust (MAT), Manchester Metropolitan University (MMU) and the Salvation Army, found that:

- Debts of up to £60,000 might be common amongst problem gamblers.
- Understanding of problem gambling amongst money advice agencies and in the NHS is extremely low.
- Awareness of the help available to problem gamblers amongst these agencies and in the NHS, particularly GPs, is equally poor.
- There is an urgent need to improve education about gambling for young people, alongside or as part of work on financial literacy and understanding chance and risk.

GamCare Chief Executive Andy McLellan said:

'The way in which we and our partners in this research came together to tackle the problem shows that there is a commitment to being joined-up, and demonstrates the importance of co-operation rather than competition between agencies. We must and will build on this. A theme of our annual conference on 19th October (which coincides with the gambling industry's Responsible Gambling Awareness Day) is about much closer working between third sector agencies and with the NHS.

'But it's not just talk:

- 'We have already run a pathfinder exercise to improve awareness amongst GPs and other agencies in some areas, and have proposals ready to go to spread this across the country as soon as funds are available.
- 'We have established a new post – Head of Education Development – to develop a practical and sustainable approach to education. We are talking to the Department for Children, Families and Schools as well and will also draw in the Youth Justice Service and other youth agencies.
- 'Our advisers and counsellors already work closely with debt advisers to ensure gamblers get the help they need, when they need it.'

Money Advice Trust Chief Executive Joanna Elson said:

'This is ground-breaking work because very little research exists about the links between problem debt and problem gambling. A practical outcome of this work is the development of a simple "screen" that advice agencies might use to help them identify when problem gambling is a cause of debt. This will help us with our vision: reducing the number of people with unmanageable debt.'

The research report also recommended:

- Action for banks and the credit industry, including publicising helplines.
- Linking with the Youth Justice Service and the criminal justice system.
- A joined-up approach to self-exclusion within the gambling industry.
- Improving awareness amongst employers of problem gamblers and the measures they can take to help their employees, e.g. using blocking software to prevent employees from gambling at work.

GamCare and the Money Advice Trust will be holding a series of meetings with key players to follow these ideas through.

14 October 2009

- The above information is reprinted with kind permission from GamCare. Visit www.gamcare.org.uk for more information.

GAMCARE

Britain's new addicts: women who gamble online, at home and in secret

A new generation are hooked on betting websites and many are unaware of where to go for help.

By Tracy McVeigh

When Kath dropped her two boys off at their primary school, she had the day to herself. But the school day was not long enough and it was when she arrived late to pick them up for the third day in a row, for the third week in a row, that the crunch came.

'The teacher called me in and said my youngest son was starting to get panicky around home time and that he had been crying when I was late. She was asking if there were any problems at home and I just felt irritated by her; I felt that she was interfering,' she said. 'Then I got home and all the anger turned to embarrassment, it all flooded over me and I was shaking and crying. It was like an emotional cold turkey, but it was still a while before I got to the point when I rang the Samaritans.'

Within a fortnight she had lost £1,700 and within a year had five-figure credit card debts that she still hasn't told her husband about

Suicidal thoughts are not uncommon in women with addictions, but Kath's was not drink or drugs, but gambling. She spent the day playing online poker. One of the fast-growing group of women turning to what has in the past been a man's game, Kath was lonely with her husband working long hours running his own business in Leeds and first tried online poker when she was 'feeling old and fed up'. Within a fortnight she had lost £1,700 and within a year had five-figure credit card debts that she still hasn't told her husband about. 'It's very numbing, you really get lost and don't snap out of it. It feels like you're on medication. Now that I'm getting counselling, it feels as if I've woken up.'

But Kath is unusual. Even as online gambling is becoming hugely popular with women who would not dream of walking into a betting shop or going alone to a casino, the numbers of women coming forward for help is not keeping pace. The situation has led Dr Henrietta Bowden-Jones, consultant psychiatrist at the National Problem Gambling Clinic in London's Soho, the only such NHS unit, to launch a child-minding service this month in an attempt to encourage more women to seek help.

'We know there is a significant impact on children of gamblers and it's difficult for women with children to get to a clinic,' said Bowden-Jones. 'So we hoped offering this service might bring more women out of the isolation, the shame and the guilt that they might be enduring alone, hidden away at home.

'The women we see are across the social spectrum, low income to high income. Losing £1,000 for one woman is equal to losing £100,000 for another. Often you are addressing people who are quite hurt and damaged and are self-medicating with gambling.'

Natasha Dow Schull, a cultural anthropologist at the Massachusetts Institute of Technology, has written a book on compulsive gambling, to be published this year. She says the mechanical rhythm of electronic gambling – slot and video poker machines – pulls players into a trance-like state, the 'machine zone', in which daily worries fade away. But it's different for men and women – men gamble for a cocaine-like rush, women for a methadone-like numbness.

'This isn't like buying shoes,' she said. 'These are potent and powerful devices effective in shifting your inner mood and state.' Her research found several incidents of women neglecting children while they gambled, including cases of babies left to die in over-heated cars parked outside casinos.

The Gambling Commission estimates that there are between 236,000 and 378,000 problem gamblers in Britain, but Gamblers Anonymous thinks it is nearer 600,000. A GA spokesman said: 'Recovery from a gambling addiction is as difficult as you want to make it. You have to want to get better and that's the same if you are male or female. We don't differentiate, we never say no to anyone who wants to recover.'

Evidence indicates that the number of women with problems has doubled in recent years, and they now make up a quarter of addicts, although when it comes to online gambling the proportion is thought to be far higher. The explosion in Internet gambling sites attracts more women than the traditionally male-dominated betting shops and casinos.

THE GUARDIAN

Charities helping compulsive gamblers report significant increases in women callers, although Ian Semel of Breakeven.org.uk said that their biggest success in getting women to come forward was with an online help site. 'Women are 50/50 with the men there; they definitely feel safer looking for help online than ringing on the phone line. The numbers are far higher than anyone admits, not helped by the fact that it is the gambling industry that provides most of the money for the help groups. It's not great that reading a message about how to deal with your addiction links back to a gambling website.'

There are an estimated 2,000 gambling websites

The British Medical Association wants gambling to be a recognised addiction in the NHS, and the money the gambling industry, through the Responsibility in Gambling Trust, pays into treatment programmes – £3.6m in 2007 – raised to at least £10m annually.

Addiction counsellor Liz Karter, who works with the charity GamCare and helped set up some of the first help groups for women compulsive gamblers, thinks it is still too early to see women coming forward with online gambling issues: 'When it comes to women, we often see gambling as a symptom of someone's underlying emotional distress,' she said.

'You do see from time to time a woman coming forward who is using gambling as a means of escape from the stresses that modern life puts on her, the demands of a job, children, her partner, her financial responsibilities. Gambling isn't like alcohol, where you can't hide being drunk and you can't look after the kids. But more often I see women who have had some traumatic experience, like an abusive relationship, and they feel quite bad about themselves so they shut everything out by gambling. You hear them say "I'm in a bubble, I'm in a trance."

'Most of the women I have been seeing are fruit machine players; we're just beginning to see the online players coming forward. But often it's not until women are in complete financial desperation that they'll finally look for help and that can be ten years down the line.'

Casino and poker websites are attracting women with 'female-friendly' gimmicks – including Barbie-pink colour schemes, 'hunk of the month' pin-ups and gambling horoscopes.

There are an estimated 2,000 gambling websites, and more are exploiting the fact that women feel safer playing online. The age profile for female online gamblers is 25 to 34, according to a Gambling Commission survey. Cashcade, which runs getmintedbingo.com, says it has an 80% female audience. Gambling sites say they have safeguards to protect against addiction. 'We have daily, weekly and monthly limits to prohibit huge spending,' said a Cashcade spokesman.

Bowden-Jones said some women were playing up to ten hours a day online. 'Women are playing online when their partners are at work, then shut down the web when their husbands come home. It's made easy for you as long as you have a credit card.

'There are sites that are targeting women. But the children are placed in front of the TV so the children are not getting the emotional nurturing.'

American author Marilyn Lancelot first visited a casino in 1984, aged 53. She describes herself as a 'recovering compulsive gambler'. Her betting led to her embezzling from her employer and serving two years in jail. 'I lost my job, home, life savings, my retirement and my freedom,' she said. She is still paying back the money and writing help books. She helped set up one of the few Internet support newsletters and forums specifically dedicated to women.

'Women have taken second place in most areas for many years and are just beginning to make a mark with the gambling addiction,' she said.

The age profile for female online gamblers is 25 to 34, according to a Gambling Commission survey

'Ten years ago there were a handful of women gambling and the few who sought out treatment were chased away by the men, either humiliated or hit on. That has changed with more women earning an income, raising families without a spouse, freedom to enter gambling establishments without an escort, and thus creating more female gamblers.

'Men usually gamble because they have large egos and are seeking power from winning in competitive games such as cards, whereas the women have low self-esteem and feel a sense of empowerment when they gamble.'

For women like Kath, the road to recovery is difficult when temptation is there every time they use a computer. 'It did occur to me to get rid of the wi-fi,' said Kath, 'but then my husband would want to know why.'

This article was amended on 22 January 2010 to remove an inaccurate quote from Liz Karter.

⇨ This article first appeared in *The Observer*, 17 January 2010.

Study indicates gambling problems linked to mental disorders

Information from CasinoGamblingWeb.com.

Hong Kong is one of the cities in the world where the largest number of gamblers reside. A new study has come out which indicates that most gambling addicts in the city also have some other form of mental disorder.

The Tung Wah Group of Hospitals, the Divisions of Addictions for Harvard Medical School and the Department of Applied Social Science of Hong Kong Polytechnic University have conducted a joint study in which they spent nine months interviewing and collecting information from 201 gamblers. The subjects were all problem gamblers who sought help for their addiction.

Over 60 per cent of the subjects were diagnosed during the time they were studied as having at least one mental disorder. The disorders ranged from depression to anxiety, and have been linked to gambling addiction in the past. The results caused the researchers to push for more mental health help.

'Mental health has long been neglected,' said Professor Daniel Shek Tan-lei of Hong Kong PolytechnicUniversity. 'But pathological gambling cannot be taken at face value. It is intertwined with psychiatric problems which must be dealt with by professionals.'

Problem gambling has reached heightened levels in recent years in Hong Kong thanks to the casino industry in Macau. The Asian gambling centre has caused many Hong Kong residents to visit, and these high-rollers sometimes fall into a betting pattern that is unhealthy.

'Pathological gambling cannot be taken at face value. It is intertwined with psychiatric problems which must be dealt with by professionals'

All across the world, doctors have been researching what could be the underlying factors that contribute to gambling addiction. Treatment centres have become commonplace in areas where casinos and other forms of gambling are prevalent. In the US some states even require treatment facilities and educational tools before the casinos are built.

The study also concluded what those before it have found, that problem gamblers are often withdrawn from their family and their loved ones. Depression and anxiety are primary causes for the withdrawal, and researchers believe that the gambling addiction only makes the mental disorders stronger.

5 September 2010

⇨ Information from CasinoGamblingWeb.com. Visit www.casinogamblingweb.com

CASINOGAMBLINGWEB.COM

Gambling addict sues casino for losses

Tycoon who blew £1.3m in 28 minutes claims he was lured back to the tables.

By Kathy Marks

Many a high-roller has lost his shirt at Melbourne's Crown casino, the largest gambling establishment in the southern hemisphere, but none, perhaps, in quite so spectacular a fashion as Harry Kakavas, who dropped 2.3 million Australian dollars (£1.3m) in one 28-minute baccarat session.

During a 15-month spree at Crown, Mr Kakavas, a multi-millionaire property dealer, turned over a total of A$1.5bn, betting up to A$300,000 a hand and ultimately losing A$20m. Now he is suing the casino – which is owned by James Packer, son of the late Kerry, himself a legendary gambler – claiming it lured him back to its tables despite knowing he was an addict.

During a 15-month spree at Crown, Mr Kakavas... turned over a total of A$1.5bn, betting up to A$300,000 a hand and ultimately losing A$20m

The Victorian Supreme Court, expected to hand down judgement imminently, heard that the casino flew Mr Kakavas to and from his home on the Queensland Gold Coast in its private jet and gave him gift-wrapped boxes containing up to A$50,000 of 'lucky money'.

This happened, according to the evidence, after Mr Packer Snr spotted Mr Kakavas in 2004 in Las Vegas, where he had just lost A$4m. Mr Packer – who once reportedly offered to toss a coin with a Texan oil magnate for the latter's US$60m (£36.8m) fortune – telephoned Crown's chief operating officer, John Williams, to ask who Mr Kakavas was and why he was not playing at Crown.

In fact, the property dealer had voluntarily excluded himself from the casino in the 1990s and sought treatment for a gambling problem. However, he had continued gambling elsewhere, although he gradually excluded himself or was banned from almost every casino in Australia.

After Mr Packer's call, Crown executives decided to readmit Mr Kakavas, although they knew – according to his lawyer, Allan Myers, QC – that 'when he got going at Crown, he could not stop'. That was literally so on one occasion, when he gambled non-stop for 17 hours, caught a few hours' sleep, then hit the tables again.

Mr Kakavas, who is suing Crown for A$30m in losses and damages, told the court: 'I don't know what [*Guinness World Records*] say, but it would be pretty close [to a world record loss].'

Crown disputes Mr Kakavas was an addict. The company, which is counter-suing him for A$1m, argues that he made his own choices. After banning himself, Mr Kakavas repeatedly lobbied Crown to be allowed back. Mr Williams described the A$2.3m loss in one sitting as not unusual for recreational gambling by a businessman.

Note: Harry Kakavas eventually lost his case to Crown Casino.
17 October 2009

Types of youth gamblers

Note: DSM-IV screen used to identify gambler types through questionnaire.

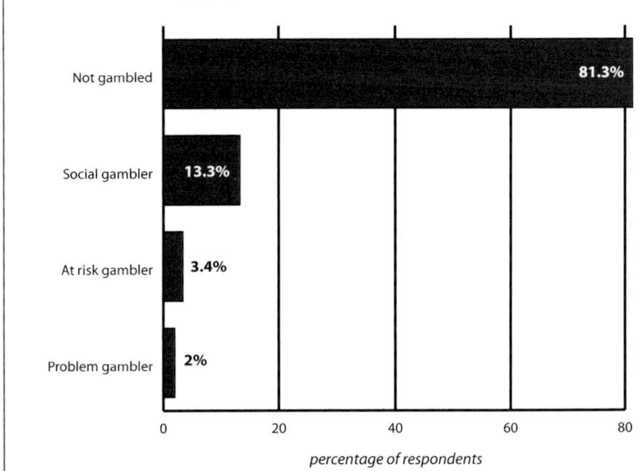

Base: Respondents aged 10–15 (n=8,958) Fieldwork dates: November 2008–February 2009

Awareness of gambling advertising

Responses to the question: 'Have you seen any adverts or pop-ups for [National Lottery and other gambling like poker, bingo and sports betting] on TV or on the Internet recently?'

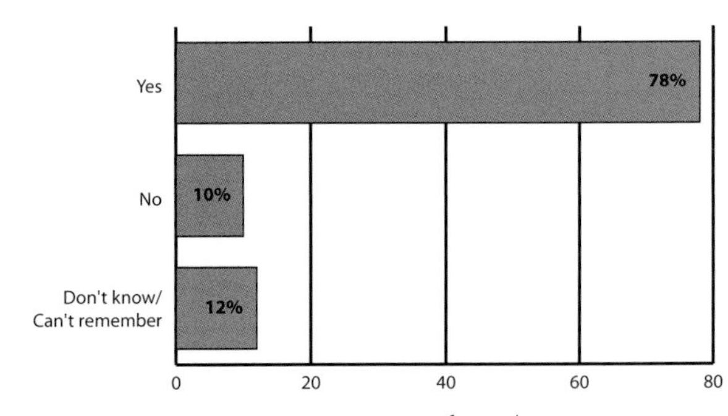

Source: British Survey of Children, the National Lottery & Gambling 2008–09, © *Ipsos MORI*

THE INDEPENDENT

Four kinds of compulsive gamblers identified

Information from SINC.

Disorganised and emotionally unstable, poorly adapted, suffering from alcohol problems, impulsive, or with a 'globally adapted' personality. These are the features of the four diagnosed types of compulsive gamblers identified by researchers at the University Hospital of Bellvitge (IDIBELL) and the Autonomous University of Barcelona (UAB). According to the scientific team, only one of these four shows signs of a significant pathology.

'We need to use different treatments for each sub-group of pathological gamblers in order to respond to their specific therapeutic difficulties and needs,' Susana Jiménez Murcia, co-author of the study and coordinator of the Pathological Gambling Unit at the Bellvitge-IDIBELL Hospital in Barcelona, tells SINC (Scientific Information and News Service).

The results of the study, which has been published in *The Canadian Journal of Psychiatry*, show that it is possible to distinguish four groups of pathological gamblers based on their personality traits and associated psychopathology.

According to the researchers, who studied 1,171 people, types I and II are pathological gamblers who exhibit problems in controlling their responses, 'but only type II shows signs of a significant concurrent psychopathology', with high levels of impulsiveness and sensation-seeking.

It is possible to distinguish four groups of pathological gamblers based on their personality traits and associated psychopathology

Resisting the urge to gamble

Pathological gambling has been defined as a progressive and chronic collapse in the ability to resist the urge to gamble. It is a kind of behaviour that damages and harms personal, family and career-related goals (APA, 2000). In mental illness manuals, pathological gambling is classified as a 'disruption in the ability to control impulses'.

'However, this classification has generated a certain degree of polemic among the scientific community, due to the high degree of heterogeneity that exists in this disorder,' the researcher explains.

For this reason, the scientific community is now looking into the possibility of introducing a new diagnostic category called 'behavioural and substance addictions' in the new editions of manuals such as the *Quinto Manual Diagnóstico y Estadístico de los Trastornos Mentales (DSM-5)* (*Fifth Diagnostic and Statistical Manual of Mental Disorders*).

Four kinds of compulsive gamblers

Type I, which could be called 'disorganised and emotionally unstable', is characterised by schizotypal personality traits, high degrees of impulsiveness, alcohol and substance abuse, psychopathological alterations and early onset age.

Type II, which is a schizoid type, exhibits high levels of harm avoidance, social distancing and alcohol abuse.

Type III is reward-sensitive, and is characterised by high levels of sensation-seeking and impulsiveness, although without any psychopathological alterations.

Type IV is a high functioning, globally-adapted personality type, without any disorders relating to substance abuse, and no associated psycho-pathological alterations.

14 October 2010

⇨ The above information is reprinted with kind permission from the Scientific and Information News Service (SINC): www.plataformasinc.es

SCIENTIFIC AND INFORMATION NEWS SERVICE

KEY FACTS

➪ Problem gambling is when harm occurs because of gambling. This harm may take many forms and can extend to other people in the gambler's life.(page 1)

➪ When thinking about gambling it is important to recognise that uncontrolled gambling causes more than just financial harm. It may also negatively affect other aspects of a gambler's life. (page 2)

➪ Over the year to September 2010 (that is, an average of figures for December 2009, March 2010, June 2010 and September 2010), 54.3% of 7,000 adults surveyed said they had participated in at least one form of gambling in the previous four weeks.(page 3)

➪ Gambling via a computer, laptop or handheld device was the most popular form of remote gambling (9.5% of all respondents), followed by gambling via mobile phone (2.7%) and interactive/digital TV (1.4%). (page 4)

➪ People between the ages of 16 and 24 are four times more likely to develop a gambling problem than any other age group. (page 6)

➪ 2% of adolescents – 60,000 12- to 15-year-olds – are problem gamblers. Yet only 5% of parents would stop their child from gambling. (page 11)

➪ Rates of gambling on commercial and non-commercial forms of gambling have fallen over time. One-fifth (21%) of children had gambled (on any type of game) in the past seven days, down from 26% in 2005–06 (according to the *British survey of children, the National Lottery and gambling*). (page 12)

➪ Survey results have indicated that parental influence and behaviour plays a key role in underage participation in gambling but that parents may be less likely to discuss gambling with their children than other potentially risky behaviours. (page 13)

➪ Asian children were no more likely than white and black children to gamble, but Asian children who gambled were more likely to be problem gamblers. (page 14)

➪ Problem gambling doesn't just affect adults. There are an estimated 127,500 people aged under 24 with a gambling problem in the UK. (page 15)

➪ The cause of a gambling problem is the individual's inability to control the gambling. This may be due in part to a person's genetic tendency to develop addiction, their ability to cope with normal life stress and even their social upbringing and moral attitudes towards gambling. (page 19)

➪ The amount of money lost or won does not determine when gambling becomes a problem. Gambling becomes a problem when it causes a negative impact on any area of the individual's life. (page 20)

➪ UK research shows that a very small percentage of people who gamble recreationally go on to develop a problem or are adversely affected by it. (page 21)

➪ Across the world problem gambling seems to be more common in men – but this might just be because women gamble less than men. (page 23)

➪ Research has shown that Cognitive Behavioural Therapy can reduce the number of days a person gambles, reduce the amount of money they lose and help a gambler stay away from gambling once they have stopped. (page 24)

➪ One study, carried out by the University of Missouri and the Queensland Institute of Medical Research, suggests there is a genetic component to gambling addiction that can be present in both men and women. (page 30)

➪ Age, gender, class, ethnicity and even geography are all likely to influence the cultures of different groups of gamblers. (page 32)

➪ Evidence indicates that the number of women with gambling problems has doubled in recent years, and they now make up a quarter of addicts, although when it comes to online gambling the proportion is thought to be far higher. (page 35)

➪ In a Hong Kong study, over 60 per cent of 201 problem gamblers were diagnosed as having at least one other mental disorder during the time that they were studied. (page 37)

➪ It is possible to distinguish four groups of pathological gamblers based on their personality traits and associated psychopathology. (page 39)

GLOSSARY

Casino

A casino is an entertainment venue where various forms of gambling are offered. Casinos may include tables for games such as poker and roulette, as well as fruit machines. Bets are placed with chips (small plastic discs used to represent money). Chips can be bought and exchanged for money on entering and leaving the casino.

Fruit machine

Fruit or slot machines are often found in pubs and casinos. Players insert money and are required to match symbols (usually fruit) in order to win the jackpot.

Gambling

An activity in which one or more persons take part, where a 'stake' (most often money) is placed on the result of an event whose outcome is uncertain. Examples include betting on sporting events, lotteries, bingo or card games.

The Gambling Commission

The regulatory authority for gambling in the UK. The Gambling Commission was set up under the Gambling Act 2005, as an independent non-departmental public body to assist with compliance and enforcement of UK gambling licensing regulations. It is supported by the Department for Culture, Media and Sport.

Lottery

A lottery is a form of gambling based purely on chance. Numbers are drawn at random from a set range, and customers win if their pre-chosen numbers match the ones that are drawn. A fee is charged to enter the lottery and the jackpot is a percentage of the amount paid by entrants.

Online gambling

Placing bets or taking part in casino games over the Internet. Internet gambling can be more dangerous than traditional forms, as players are easily able to transfer large amounts of cash without leaving their home. Since the money is transferred electronically, it can seem less 'real' and debts build up more easily.

Problem gambling

When gambling becomes an addiction that starts to have a noticeable negative impact on someone's life, this is referred to as 'problem gambling'. It might affect relationships, employment or someone's financial situation: for example, they may acquire heavy debts, and the secretive nature of their addiction may put a strain on family relationships.

Remote gambling

Placing bets by remote means: for example, using a mobile phone or computer. The term 'remote' refers to the fact that players do not need to enter a bookmakers or casino to place their bet; they can gamble from any location.

Spread betting

Spread betting is a high-risk form of gambling, where the odds are not fixed but fluctuate. Spread betting can be used on sporting events or the stock market, and involves wagering on a range (or spread) of outcomes rather than a fixed 'win or lose'. It reduces the control the gambler has over the amount that they lose, although for the same reason, winnings can be very large.

ACKNOWLEDGEMENTS

The publisher is grateful for permission to reproduce the following material.

While every care has been taken to trace and acknowledge copyright, the publisher tenders its apology for any accidental infringement or where copyright has proved untraceable. The publisher would be pleased to come to a suitable arrangement in any such case with the rightful owner.

Chapter One: Gambling Trends

Understanding gambling, © State of Victoria, *Gambling participation*, © Gambling Commission. All rights reserved, *Types of gambling,* © Gamble Aware, *What is gambling?,* © GamCare, *FAQ: gambling and you*, © TheSite.org, *Why a healthy brain is no good for gambling*, © Guardian News and Media Limited 2010, *Gambling on the up, says Sportingbet*, © Associated Newspapers Limited 2010.

Chapter Two: Young People and Gambling

Youth gambling and problem gambling, © International Centre for Youth Gambling Problems and High-Risk Behaviors, *Kids speak out about gambling*, © International Centre for Youth Gambling and High-Risk Behaviors, *GamCare targets teen gambling*, © GamCare, *Children, the National Lottery and gambling 2008–09*, © Ipsos MORI, *Young people and problem gambling*, © GamCare, *Adolescent gambling on the Internet*, © Nottingham Trent University.

Chapter Three: Problem Gambling

FAQ: problem gamblers, © National Council on Problem Gambling, *Problem gambling – 'the hidden addiction'*, © 2010 Memiah Limited, *Problem gambling*, © Royal College of Psychiatrists, *Britain's binge-gambling problem*, © Guardian News and Media Limited 2010, *Drug treatments for adolescents with gambling problems?*, © National Center for Responsible Gaming, *Internet poker ruined my life*, © TheSite.org, *Gambling addiction linked to genes*, © Crown copyright is reproduced with the permission of Her Majesty's Stationery Office – nhs.uk, *Situating problem gambling: the social context of 'gambling careers' [research summary]*, © University of Glasgow, *Situating problem gambling: the social context of 'gambling careers' [key findings]*, © Economic and Social Research Council, *Gamblers in debt need better education and joined-up help*, © GamCare, *Britain's new addicts: women who gamble online, at home and in secret*, © Guardian News and Media Limited 2010, *Study indicates gambling problems linked to mental disorders*, © CasinoGamblingWeb.com, *Gambling addict sues casino for losses*, © The Independent, *Four kinds of compulsive gamblers identified*, © SINC.

Illustrations

Pages 1, 19, 28, 37: Angelo Madrid; pages 2, 10, 27, 34: Don Hatcher; pages 8, 25, 31, 39: Simon Kneebone; pages 15, 32: Bev Aisbett.

Cover photography

Left: © Henriette Hansen. Centre: © Lance Palmer. Right: © Michaël Spoiden.

Additional acknowledgements

Editorial and layout by Carolyn Kirby on behalf of Independence.

And with thanks to the Independence team: Mary Chapman, Sandra Dennis and Jan Sunderland.

Lisa Firth
Cambridge
January, 2011

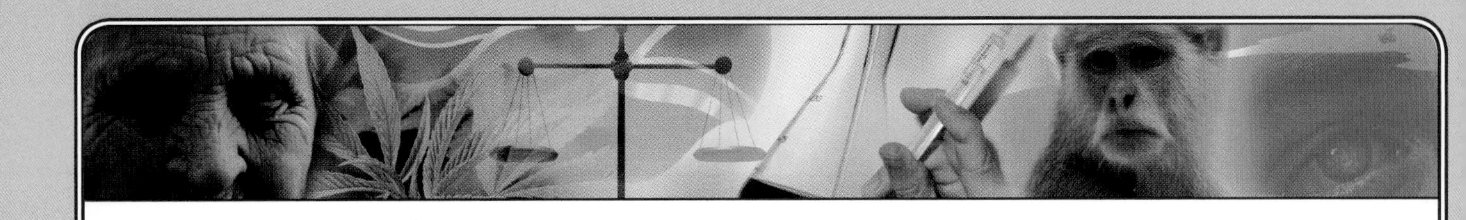

ASSIGNMENTS

The following tasks aim to help you think through the issues surrounding the gambling debate and provide a better understanding of the topic.

1 Read *Gambling participation* on pages 3–4. How valid is this research? Make a list of the measures taken by the researchers to ensure their study is a fair and accurate representation of the views of the nation as a whole (e.g. by using a nationally representative sample), with a brief description of what each measure would entail.

2 Watch the film 'Casino Royale'. Do you think this film glamourises gambling? Is it right to portray gambling as exciting and attractive to film audiences? Write a review of the film which includes your views on this moral dilemma.

3 Read *Problem gambling* on pages 23–25. Write a concise, informative booklet on the support available to problem gamblers and where they might go for help. You could use the websites of some of the organisations listed in the 'Where can I get help?' section to carry out further research.

4 Read *What is gambling?* on page 5. Create an illustrated timeline to portray the history of gambling. Choose one event on your timeline about which your knowledge is limited. Carry out further research on this event and write a detailed summary of your findings.

5 Based on the articles in this book, make a list of words and phrases that you think describe how people feel and act when they have a gambling problem. Write an emotive, empathetic poem based on your list, using an appropriate tone and style for the subject matter. Think about your choice of vocabulary and whether you will write in the first, second or third person before you begin.

6 The article on pages 12–14, *Children, the National Lottery and gambling 2008–09*, compares some of its findings with results from the 2005–06 report. Choose three of the points in the 'Key findings' section and create a graph showing the difference in findings from the two surveys.

7 'Debt and relationship problems caused through gambling are a problem gambler's own fault. They chose to gamble their money away and it's only right that they have to live with the consequences.' Debate this proposal in two groups, with one group supporting the statement and the other group arguing against it.

8 Read the newspaper article on page 38, *Gambling addict sues casino for losses*. Imagine you were the lawyer representing Harry Kakavas, and you are preparing to file the law suit against the casino. Write a summary of the arguments with which you hope to win the case.

9 Design a pop-up window for an Internet poker site, warning of the addictive nature of gambling and advising potential problem gamblers where they can go for help. The window should be eye-catching and persuasive, ensuring gamblers are aware of the potential dangers of betting websites.

10 Carry out a research investigation into gambling practices from cultures around the world. You can use the websites suggested in this book, as well as search engines to find your own sources of information. Is problem gambling only an issue in developed or western societies? Can you find any types of gambling that are not listed in this book, which are found in other countries? Write a summary of your findings.

11 In groups, present the findings of a research report featured in this book. Choose either *Gambling addiction linked to genes* (pages 30–31) or *Situating problem gambling: the social context of 'gambling careers'* (pages 32–33). Create a ten-minute PowerPoint presentation outlining what the research involved, who carried it out and what the main findings were. Illustrate your findings with graphs and tables.

12 Read the article called *Internet poker ruined my life* on pages 28–29. Write a short piece of prose in the form of a diary entry written from Jane's point of view. Imagine what Jane would do throughout her day, including her thoughts on how she feels about her situation and her fears for the future.

13 Las Vegas is considered the gambling capital of the world. Using the Internet, travel magazines and travel guides, carry out a research project into Las Vegas as a holiday destination. Is gambling used to market this destination? Is information about help for problem gambling readily available to potential tourists? Write a short report on your findings.

14 In pairs, record a radio interview on the subject of problem gambling. One of you will be the presenter and the other a problem gambling expert. Read *FAQ: gambling and you* on page 6 for some background information.